Hey Sal!

Farikanayi

Text copyright © 2013 farikanayi

All rights reserved

Author photo © Pearl Munhawa

ISBN 13:978-0957627321 (Caroline Manyika)

All bible quotes are in NIV unless otherwise stated

DEDICATION

I am dedicating this book to a couple of VIPs:
My parents Rahab and Kennedy Manyika have both been awesome role models and examples of the benefits of serving God. They kept an open invitation for their God who became our God and they included him and sought his input in every decision and every detail of their lives and ours.

Mum went home on 7th September this year, leaving a void in my life I cannot fill but which God will see me through. She was an avid reader and I hoped that she would get to read some of my books. It wasn't meant to be but I am sure she has left me enough writing material for a few books. I'm sure also that she won't stop praying for her family just because she is in now heaven!

My parents taught me to love words. Papers and pens were always available in our home as were books and encyclopaedias. It is not a surprise that my siblings and I all love reading and writing. We were taught by the best.

Contents

INTRO 1

LETTER 1 7

LETTER 2 26

LETTER 3 54

LETTER 4 64

LETTER 5 84

LETTER 6 107

LETTER 7 134

LETTER 8 158

LETTER 9 181

LETTER 10 193

LETTER 11 210

ROLE MODEL OF ROLE MODELS .. 225

LETTER 12 228

ACKNOWLEDGEMENTS

There are some places that you visit and you wax creative. Having family around you, people you don't see regularly but whose love reassures you and embraces you makes you relaxed and at such times the creative juices flow. Zimbabwe is one such place and I want to acknowledge her because this book was born and took shape on Zimbabwean soil.

I'd like to acknowledge some of the people who played a part in this book coming to completion:

My children who continue to be my source of joy and inspiration. They hold a very special place in my heart and each time I start on a project they are central to its success.

My Pastors, the various men and women God continues to use to teach me His Word so that I can increase, improve, grow and shine.

The special friends God has given me who cheer even when I feel like I have not done anything worth cheering for. They have that special discernment which makes them see and coax out of me the creativity I don't always see or know that it is there.

The Word of God which is still settled in heaven (119:89). I feed on it and receive my teaching, rebuke, correction and training in righteousness, so that I may be thoroughly equipped for every good work (2 Timothy 3:16). There is no better reference material than the BIBLE and I thank God for each verse and for his revelation of the promises and all the spiritual nutrition he has packed in it.

I thank God, my maker, my father the lifter up of my head (Psalm 3:3) who has never agreed with people's opinions of me but has lined up role models for me to learn from. He has loved me and loves me with an everlasting love (Jeremiah 31:3) and his unshifting banner over me is love (Song of Solomon 2:4) while buoying me up are his everlasting arms (Deuteronomy 33:27). Thank you Lord.

INTRO

I have been greatly blessed to have a father that I can look up to, a man who has remained my role model to this day when he is in his 90s. He is far from perfect and is as human as any other parent, but despite his inadequacies as a human father, he has been an excellent role model. He has done everything in his power to give my siblings and I what we know has been as 'normal' a childhood as anyone could have and we know beyond a shadow of doubt that we have been blessed.

Some people have brothers or sister, friends, teachers and other adults that help shape their thoughts and general life patterns. But for me, even though my parents have totally earned my respect, I still find that the role models I refer and defer to the most are the ones whose lives make up the awesome book called the bible.

The presence and accessibility of these great men and women is a clear demonstration of God's love for us. He knows our earthly family situations aren't always ideal. He knows that some parents and siblings are the cause of tears and problems faced by a lot of children, the issues that trail them into adulthood. He knows that some families are so dysfunctional that there may not be a single role model for the kids.

So in his goodness and mercy he surrounds us with such a great cloud of witnesses (Hebrews 12:1) such an array of emmulateable people that for each of us there is hope that our lives can be shaped by the influence of these amazing but also very human role models whose lives and life stories provide templates from which any life can be shaped, out of whatever challenges it may emerge from.

In these letters I identify in said perpetual role models the characteristics of them I appreciate as they set standards for living and for loving for the present generations. In them I identify what I would love to have in a life partner as I also celebrate what I admire in their relationships with their spouses and or with God and with the people around them. In these letters I don't pretend that these are perfect role models but that these are human role models who have experienced success, failure, grief, joy, pain and every emotion and experience that has been noted to be 'common to men' (1 Corinthians 13:10).

Although the letters are addressed to specific people in the bible, in essence they are highlighting Godly characteristics of men and women in this day and age who choose to become what they learn from the great 'cloud of witnesses' mentioned in Hebrews and presented to us in sixty books that make up the bible. This book is my way of saluting and celebrating every person who chooses to become a beacon of light that young children, teenagers and everyone else can see and follow or emulate.

Included are letters to Salmon, Joshua, Boaz, David, Samuel, Gideon, Caleb, Mordecai and Samson. Although these represent just a handful of role models, they are an interesting mix and cover what I will refer to as a 'conundrum of life experiences, successes and failures'.

The exciting aspect of this list is the fact that even though these are all excellent role models for this generation, they are also very human and as highly as we may praise their prowess in battle, their fairness as judges, their consistency in service and whatever other positive attributes they have, we also see their humanity revealed in their not so great choices, decisions and actions. This makes them attainable as role models as their lives highlight the evidence and activity of grace. They show that earthen vessels can despite their fragility and frailty contain and protect great treasure (2 Corinthians 4:7). They also reflect the love of God who knows each person intimately warts and all and still loves that imperfect person. He loves you and he loves me even though we know we are far from perfect. His grace remains the qualifying factor for humanity.

The list wouldn't be complete obviously without the inclusion of barrier-breaking, discrimination-busting, non-conformist Deborah who completes the line-up of role models whetting the appetite and also leaving room and the desire for the exploration of female role models in future. Alongside her are very brief summations of lessons from some wonderful mothers and sisters, people like Sarah, Tamar, Sheerah, Jael, Esther and Rahab.

The list definitely couldn't and wouldn't be complete of course without the inclusion of the role model of role models, the Wonderful Counsellor, Mighty God, Everlasting Father, Prince of Peace (Isaiah 9:6b).
No one else can match my Lord and saviour. I live to be more like him and for the prophetic word spoken

in 1 John 4:17 to become my living and evident reality:

As he is, so are we in this world

LETTER 1

Salmon, strong visionary

Overlooking opinions of men

Seeing what none else could see

Seeing beyond the ugliness of scars

To a perfection only God can bring

Seeing a wife within the harlot

The Lord's grandmother

Where many saw someone to use

HEY SAL,

I'm writing this letter to express my appreciation of the man you are, the men you represent. Maybe what you express and reveal is a natural exposé of who you are, maybe you don't need to make an effort to be the wonderful man you are. For all I know maybe you have consciously worked on your character so that in the end the man who has emerged is this wonderful person I have learned to admire, respect and look up to.

We find the story of your life chronicled without much detail in Joshua 2 and also in Matthew 1:5. The outcome of your actions gives us some insight into who you are, the man Rahab was blessed to be loved by. You don't need a lot of words or accolades. Your actions and their results speak loud and clear bringing hope and wisdom even into this generation.

There are people in my life who seem to think I'm all that. They encourage, stir and sometimes challenge the gifts in me. Yet there are times when I don't really know who they are talking about. I don't always see what seems crystal clear to them. I have now learned to allow the iron that is these special people to sharpen the iron that is me or in me (Proverbs 27:17). So maybe you may not realise or recognise the Salmon I see, the Salmon countless others hopefully see and the Salmon that I am sure

Rahab loved, appreciated, respected and valued. Allow me to speak about you, to reveal what I have learned and what I hope others will not only learn from but also emulate. Allow me also to present you as a role model for the many men who have no one to look up to in their direct network of family and friends.

Let your life continue to speak, unlimited and undiminished, unquenched by the passage of time.

Bravery

I believe that you are a really brave man and I have come to this conclusion by a process of deduction. You were sent along with another to spy the city of Jericho so that the army of Israel could invade it. I doubt if Joshua would have sent a coward, or someone who didn't have a sendable spirit. Joshua needed men who could go in, gather intelligence and get out unharmed to report back to him so that he could strategize.

By the same process of deduction I would say you are also a very intelligent man, one who can think on his feet. So many people dilly dally when important decisions need to be made. They don't have the backbone to make decisions and stand by them, they over-consult making simple issues very complicated. You obviously didn't have the benefit of time on your hands and you had to assess the situation you were in and come up with an accurate valuation quickly which you did.

I deduce also that you are a man who submits to the authority God put over your life. You were accountable to Joshua, you were a man under authority like the man we learn about in Matthew 8: 9. Because of your submissive spirit, much power was also entrusted to you so that you could make on the spot decisions like deciding to save Rahab and her family.

But from reading about your encounter with Rahab, I can tell also that you are a very decisive man. A woman feels very secure when she is connected to a man like you. You are brave, you are up for the challenges that face you, you analyse situations and make decisions quickly but also wisely. What's not to like in someone like you, what's not to like!

Wise

You obviously operated in wisdom. When you were sent to Jericho you knew the right person to approach. You needed someone who would know what was happening in Jericho. You could have asked the kids on the street, or you could have been chauvinistic in your approach by seeking out male informants just because they are male, but you were wise enough to know that Rahab by virtue of her profession would know the men in the city, the happenings in the city and possibly the secrets of the city. Her profession gave her access to all sorts of men who were vulnerable while they were in her presence and were likely to share secrets with her. You used that knowledge to choose her as your informant and what a wise choice you made.

Sometimes people exclude some people based on gender, age, race, ethnicity and some of these human and very superficial differences and demarcations. They don't give themselves the chance to know someone and what is in them because the person is black, or white, or poor or uneducated or more talented or less gifted than them. They have these fixed categories of who is acceptable and who isn't and they forget that God said that he would use the foolish things to confound the wise (1 Corinthians 1:27) and that his thoughts are not our thoughts (Isaiah 55:8).

I can just see God placing the solutions we need in the little old lady people don't talk to because she is old and is by human perceptions past her sale-by-date. As a result they spend money seeking wisdom and advice from counsellors and 'wise' people or experts when a wise though wrinkly- skinned expert is right there in their midst daily. Just because she is packaged differently than what they expect wisdom to be packaged, they lose out. As a result they miss out of sound counsellors, relationships and friendships. But you took a well calculated risk and went to Rahab. That is wisdom.

I thank God that he knows us and our human propensity to focus on packaging. Therefore he is not silent and he does not leave us to find our own way. He gives us among other scriptures, Proverbs 8 which is rich as wisdom speaks to us sharing with us her attributes:

I love those who love me, and those who seek me find me. With me are riches and honor, enduring wealth and prosperity. My fruit is better than fine gold; what I yield surpasses choice silver v17-19

…. bestowing a rich inheritance on those who love me and making their treasuries full v21.

Encouraged accountability in Rahab

One of the things I find really special about you is the fact that you encouraged Rahab to be responsible for the salvation of her family. You encouraged maturity. Many people enjoy being thanked and being praised for their good deeds. What they don't sometimes realise is the fact that their 'helping' actually cripples the people they assist. It's okay to give someone a loaf of bread if they are hungry. But then you have to make sure you give them a loaf for each proceeding day otherwise they will go hungry yet again. Sometimes it is better to give someone a piece of fabric from which they can start a tailoring business, or to give them a book from which they can glean wisdom or learn a trade, rather than crippling them with kindness by giving them left-overs, building in them a lifestyle of dependency.

You didn't do that to Rahab. You taught her accountability. She was responsible for putting an agreed upon sign outside her window (Joshua 2:17). She was also responsible for talking to her family members and making sure that they were all in her house when Jericho fell. Without this agreement Rahab would have expected you to go into the city and gather her relatives before you could destroy the city. Your life would have been in danger as would your colleagues.

Instead you wanted to relate with a mature woman who didn't think that the world owed her everything. In a way I suppose you were also preparing her for being the mother she would one day become. It's good to be a blessing, but sometimes the blessing does not have to be material, it can be in teaching someone a skill, a trade, in making the person independent rather than dependent. You did that for Rahab.

Honourable

Another aspect of your character I really value is the fact that you are a man of honour. You are a man of your word. You speak and mean what you say. The bible exhorts us to be people whose yea is yea and whose nay is also nay (James 5:12b) and this is who you are. You promised Rahab that she would be safe and you kept your word. You are a man of honour, a man whose word has weight.

Not everyone says what they mean or means what they say. Some people's mouths are like public restrooms, anything goes in and out, there is no standard, there is no expectation of real privacy or real decency. Someone has to go in after people to check that they have left it reasonably clean. Some people are like that. As soon as they open their mouths you have to launch damage control. Lies issue out, anger spews out, deceit crawls out and lives are damaged:

> *There is that speaketh like the piercings of a sword: but the tongue of the wise is health. (Proverbs 12:18 KJV)*

But your word was a word of life and to this day we see Rahab included in the list of heroes and heroines who became the ancestors of our Lord and Saviour (Hebrews 11:31; James 2:25; Matthew 1:5).

Visionary

Of all your attributes Salmon let me say that your insight, your discernment and your ability to see what others didn't or couldn't see is what I value the most about you. Rahab was a prostitute, even to this day we refer to her as Rahab the harlot. But this did not seem to faze you at all. You got to know the real woman not the harlot but the woman who was brave enough to hide you, wise enough to negotiate for her safety and generous enough to plead for the salvation of her family. You saw the strategically placed woman and appreciated what she did for you, whatever her motives were. I am so thankful that you can be a teacher to those men who want to marry but are looking for the perfect virgin who has never sinned. You teach people not to be hypocritical, not to seek from others what they are not able to give or to be. This is such a Christ-like attribute that I can only admire and appreciate.

Nowadays many people have a list of traits and characteristics of the ideal spouse they want. Yet they forget that they should also be able to fulfil or meet someone else's list. They are not introspective, they don't take time to analyse themselves to see what gives them the right to expect someone to be able to meet the thirty items on their tick-off list when maybe they only manage to tick off three of the other person's list items. They are lazy and not willing to work for what they want. Instead like the 10 spies sent to spy the Promised Land (Numbers 13) they expect a land that is peaceful, unoccupied, with fields that are already cultivated and farm animals already in pens. They don't realise that there is a level of responsibility expected of us and a certain amount of work we have to do in order to become the people God wants us to be.

No man meets a perfect woman nor does any woman meet a perfect man. Instead they have to see the positives in each other and decide whether or not this is enough for them to become a couple. They also need to realise that they have to work at their relationship just like we have to work out our salvation with fear (reverence) and trembling (Philippians 2:12). Thank you Sal for being a man of insight and for having eyes that see what God has already deposited and started in others.

Promoter of the gifts in those around you

Yet another aspect of who you are which I am grateful for is the fact that you used your name to make good happen to and for others. You gave Rahab stature, turned her circumstances from a harlot to a wife to a woman of value and importance mentioned in the bible as part of the genealogy of Christ in Matthew 1:5. Your name made her a respectable woman, a wife and a mother. This reminds of John the Baptist. He was a man of influence in his own right and he used his position and his name to announce and present Christ to the world. Christ also did the same for us as he became our substitute, he became sin yet he didn't know sin before (2 Corinthians 5:21), he became poor so that we could become rich (2 Corinthians 8:9). He poured of himself so that we could have life and have it more abundantly (John 10:10).

Many people do all they can to stifle other people's candles. They want to be the only light, the only success story, the only person on the stage. They don't realise that 2 candles shine brighter than one or that there is blessing in being a blessing. They are fame and wealth hoarders. But this is obviously not the sort of man you are. You are obviously the type of leader who wants the limelight to fall on you and those around you. You are not intimidated by the prosperity of others because you know this does not detract from your own prosperity and success. When God lifts you up, like Christ you also draw others up with you (John 12:32). What a blessing to be a selfless giver, to be like Abraham who was told that through him the whole earth would be blessed (Genesis 18:18; Genesis 22:18; Genesis 12:3). You are like those mentioned in (Isaiah 52:7; Romans 10:15) who are blessed, whose feet bring good news to others. You brought love, family, stature, motherhood, wealth and your good name to Rahab. Thank you. May those who have been blessed in whatever way learn from you and use their blessing to bless others and to cause good to happen to them. I pray also that whatever God brings into my hands does not end there but is distributed to bless those around me who may be in greater need than I am.

On a personal note Sal, I hope you don't mind me calling you Sal, it's not because I am disrespecting you, it is because I feel like I know you a bit after studying your life. One of the reasons why I really appreciate the man you are is that you loved a woman who in many ways reminds me of myself. You loved a woman who was despised by others because of life choices she made, been there. You loved a woman who must have been a topic for many conversations even among the children of Israel, been there. You loved a woman who though obviously intelligent made some poor choices in life, been there.

You loved a woman who may have despised herself may not have thought highly of herself, also been there. You demonstrated the sort of love our Lord and Savour also demonstrated when he loved us while we were yet sinners (Roams 5:8). You gave hope to the hopeless. How can I not love appreciate and respect a man like that, a visionary like that?

My prayer is for the men whose lives cross mine to have your vision and your strength. I pray that they may see me and see the people around them the way God sees them. As they seek a marriage partner, may they not be blinded by the obvious, but rather seek the sought after female value described in Proverbs 31. I pray that they seek the wisdom of

God more than they seek to please their peers. I pray also that they will not be hypocrites, men of double standards expecting from others what they can't provide or be, expecting to marry a virgin when they themselves are a well-travelled road.

Thank you for being a man whose character brings hope to those of us who have needed a second, third or even fourth chance, those of us who like Rahab fell off the straight and narrow and became what others discuss and despise. Thank you for despising the fickle standards of men and going totally against the grain to cause the desolate places to be inhabited again (Ezekiel 36:35; Isaiah 54:3) and settling the barren woman in her own home (Psalm 113:9).

Thank you Sal, I call forth your sons, those men whose character reflects yours. I call them from the North and South from the East and also from the West (Isaiah 43:6). Let them flood our nations, our churches and our lives. Let them step up like you and take responsibility, even risks, to ensure that it is well with their wives, sisters, children, mothers, nations and their generation. Let them come and lead in the knowledge and the fear of the Lord the way real men should, let them come and lead like you.

Love and blessings

Fari

LETTER 2

HEY JOSH,

Josh I have to say this upfront; I speak your name by faith. I call those things that be not as though they are as it says in (Romans 4:17). When I pray for my husband-to-be or the men I want in my life as friends, brothers, business contacts, I call forth Joshua, not you but a man like you because I both respect and admire you greatly. The book of Joshua is rich with details of your character, your actions, your victories and the challenges you both faced and overcame.

Actually the real reason why you have become the epitome, the essence of husband/lover/friend/life-partner to me is because I know myself well. I know the kind of people I want around me not just in marriage but even in friendship and any other kind of connection. I know who I used to be and I know the sort of people I used to gravitate towards, but that era of my life is gone. God has revealed it to me that his grace is sufficient for me (2 Corinthians 12:9) and that he has given me all sufficiency and ensured that I will abound unto all good works, not just average works, not just little works, but all good works (2 Corinthians 9:8).

To be able therefore to become who God says I am, I also have to make sure that running alongside me are people in a similar race. I don't want to set off on my life-time journey running alongside the Jamaican Usain Bolt, he would wear me out before I accomplished what God wants me to do. I don't want to run alongside the Ethiopian long distance runner Haile Selassie if what I need to do requires me to sprint, he would drag out what needs to be done now! So now that there is clarity regarding my vision, there also has to be clarity regarding my running mates and I don't want or need any unfocussed person, I don't need any head-on-one –side-pity-party person, nor do I need people who are happy to just go with the flow.

I have been called stubborn by my mother and my brothers and I used to hate this tag but now I realise that that tenacity has allowed me to live where I should have died and that stubbornness has kept me sane where I could have lost my mind. I know that strength has kept me going when I could easily have given up and despaired. God equipped me for the storms that were brewing but which I didn't see. My family didn't know the wars I would need to go through, nor did they know the battles I was already embroiled in even while I was a little girl. But God saw and despite what was happening in my life, he gave me fortitude, contradictory fortitude because I did not appear strong. He sustained me and built me up, buffeting me from storms that could have destroyed my life then finally planted my feet securely and said:

My grace is sufficient for you, for my power is made perfect in weakness 2 Corinthians 12:9

So I now know who I am and I know that the man, friend, partner I would click with, the one that would live or work peaceably with me would be someone like you, a strong man, a winner, a man with a vision and focus who wouldn't be put off by who I am as a woman, or who I am as a woman who now refuses to be mediocre or to operate below God's expectations for me, for who he has made me to be.

Going against the grain

One of the saddest things to witness is young people wanting to be different but at the same time copying what everyone else does. There is this complexity in their character and attitude toward life which leaves parents perplexed. They rebel yet conform.

They disobey yet obey. They want to stand out yet blend in.

But you didn't seem to have this paradox in your character. It didn't matter to you about being in the majority. You wanted to do what was right even if it meant that you were the only one doing it. You wanted to follow God and to follow your leader Moses even if no one else did. In a way I believe this is why God didn't allow you to be defiled but removed you from the congregation when they made that golden calf (Exodus 32). You were with Moses at that time. You are both a trendsetter and a trail blazer, both submissive and in authority. You have what God describes as a different spirit (Numbers 14:24). I really want to be like that, to do what's right even when it is not fashionable.

I hope our daughters, the young ladies living in this generation learn from you that it is right to be a virgin even if you are the only one in your whole circle of friends. Let the young man know that it is okay to serve God even if your friends and peers laugh at you, that is honourable not to go around deflowering girls then expect to marry a virgin. I pray that fathers learn that it is good to love their families and spend quality time even if no one else does, even if everyone else spends all hours on the job, in the pub, the club and wherever else but home.

So as I have analysed and studied the many men in the word of God so that I know what sort of husband to pray for, for myself, for my children and for the many single women whose lives are linked to mine, you keep coming top of the list. For this reason I need to let you know what it is about you that makes my heart flutter, what it is about you that makes me sit and assess your attributes so that I can identify them in THE man I am going to share the rest of my earthy life with.

Overcomer

I love the fact that you were always prepared to fight and overcome all obstacles. You did not lose a single battle bar when Achan disobeyed God and stole a Babylonian robe, silver and gold (Joshua 7). Your level of bravery remains a record that is unbroken. I am not implying that all men should go and join the army, a physical army. But every man should make the people in his life know that they are safe and secure. He should be prepared to fight to make sure that whatever God has said the family must have becomes a reality. God does not want his people to be poor. So if a family is facing poverty and lack, someone needs to rise up and fight the poverty giants and make sure that the family ends up taking the territory denied them by the giants. If a family is facing sickness, foolishness, sin, addictions, strife or whatever giants are standing in their way, their victory must come through the man who refuses to be affected by these enemies and wages full-blown war on them so that his family is secure.

How sad is it when a man hides behind his wife, girlfriend or children and expects them to fight so that he can have the things that are lacking for the family. That sort of role reversal makes life hard for the family and brings total confusion as roles are redefined to accommodate the cowardly man who can't fight and overcome the enemies his family faces.

My friend will forgive me for using this example. I went to visit one of my friends and he picked me up from the train station. As we walking off towards the car park a man came towards us with a dog on a leash. Now I am a bit scared of dogs having been bitten by one at my parents' house. I wasn't too worried on this occasion because I had a big man with me so I felt safe. Well next thing I knew hands were holding my shoulders from behind me! My friend who is a foot or so taller than me and way broader was hiding behind me because he has a dog phobia! Had the dog wanted to get him he still could as I wasn't hiding much of him because of our difference is size.

I laugh now when I look back to that incident because I know this friend of mine is not cowardly. He is a hard-working man who is an excellent provider for his family. But his behaviour on that day made me realise the ridiculousness of a man who hides behind the people he should be providing for, stretching forth his hand, usually with attitude and violence when he should be giving and providing for their needs.

But looking over the events of your life Josh I can see that you were not that kind of man. You knew that in order to possess what the Lord had promised you, you needed to fight and overcome the enemy and that is precisely what you did. You didn't shirk your responsibilities, you didn't expect others to do what God had placed before you to be done; you refused to be a 'kept' man.

I pray that men who read the book of Joshua don't just skirt over your battles and scan through but take time to really read about your life and to learn from you what a good man does and is.

God's vision

I believe that the thing that made it possible for you to overcome is the fact that you allowed your eyes to see what God saw and sees. You refused to be myopic, you refused to operate in the natural or to rely on the arm of flesh (2 Chronicles 32:8; Philippians 3:3; Psalm 44:6; Proverbs 3:5).

What you did instead was to find out what God said, and what God expected of and for the children of Israel. I suppose for marriages, relationships and ministries to work people need to have a pattern, they need to know what God expects and they need to know what is acceptable and what should not be tolerated. Thankfully God has not left us ignorant or left us to flounder as we try to figure this out. He spells things out in his word if we take time to read and meditate (Joshua 1:8) and hide the word in our hearts so that we don't sin against him (Psalm 119:11) by doing things wrong and initiating some dubious and weird templates of marriage and relationships. You only need to turn a television set on or open a newspaper to see some of the crazy things people have accepted and embraced as normal.

God's vision for all aspects of our life is spelt out in his word. I now understand what the instruction you were given in Joshua 1:8 means when God presented to you what he referred to as the 'book of the law'. In your days you only had a few books but as you know over time God continued to speak and faithful people recorded his love letters to us so that we now have a more comprehensive presentation of God's instructions for us. How awesome for us that you became part of the material God wanted future generations to access and learn from.

We therefore have no excuse for not knowing God's will for us regarding our lives, our families, our marriages and everything that affects us in any way. He has given us the outlines and the content of the doctrine we should be steeped in (2 Timothy 3:16) Added to the clear instructions in his word God has also made sure that he still comes to fellowship with us as he inhabits our praise (Psalm 22:3) and also through taking residence within us through his Holy Spirit who is our counsellor and teacher (11 John 2:27; John 14:26) and who is also God's power in us (2 Timothy 1:7; Acts 1:8) and our comforter (John 15:26). He is also referred to as the Spirit of truth who will guide us in all truth (John 16:13). So in addition to the clarity brought by his written word, we also have our own internal guide who is ever present to help us see as God sees.

Even though you lived in the dispensation way before where I am now where the Holy Spirit dwells within us and speaks to and through us, you still heard from the Lord and you still leaned on him and boldly went forward to fight the enemy that was standing in the way of your inheritance. The bible says that God teaches our hands to war and our fingers to do battle (Psalm 144:1KJV), how I wish today's man would gird his loins with strength (1 Peter 1:13; Exodus 12:11) and set his face like flint (Isaiah 50:7; Ezekiel 3:9) and fight confusion, foolishness, addictions, strife, sinfulness, lust, poverty, divorce, rebellion and all the giants fighting against families stopping them from living in the Shalom intended for them.

How I pray that his hands would bring wealth, comfort, love and gentle caresses to his family rather than be clenched into fists that inflict pain and instil fear. That he would know that the battles God teaches us to be involved in are not against our loved ones, they are against the enemies, the giant occupants of our inheritance, our promised land (Ephesians 6:12). There is nothing friendly about pain and death caused by someone who should be loving and nurturing you. So I thank you Joshua for teaching us what it is to overcome, for refusing to authenticate 'friendly fire' and for making clear the difference between the enemy and the family.

Fighting to the end

Some people start off well and with good intentions but they give up before they reach the end line. You could have done the same. You could have fought for your own family's inheritance making sure all the Nuns (Joshua 1:1) had their land. You could then have stepped back and enjoyed the land God had given you. But you were like the builder (Luke 14:28) who counted the cost before starting on his construction but made preparations to see the project to the end. You were not like those men who show interest in a woman but give up when the first argument arises or when a problem occurs. They don't have staying power or relational stamina. As soon as things get tough they are the weaklings that also get going. You are not like the women who pack their bags as soon as things don't go their way, or as soon as a little difficulty crops up.

You started fighting when Moses died, you took up the baton and you did not stop running till you reached the end, till every enemy had been destroyed. I pray that the men in my circle would be like you; that my friends, sons, uncles, cousins and brothers would be men that can be relied on to fight to the end till every enemy has been defeated, till the battle is won, till the fat lady has sung.

God's instructions followed and accomplished

As I read the book of Joshua and also the other parts of the bible where you are mentioned, I realise that one of the reasons why you succeeded in all you did was the fact that you followed God's instructions to a T. You heard what Moses said regarding the Promised Land and you also heard what God said to you. That became your template for everything you did. You didn't try to change the modus operandi to something you thought would be better, but instead kept the book of the law, your instruction manual, before your eyes always and determined not to divert, detour or deviate from it:

> *This book of the law shall not depart out of thy mouth; but thou shalt meditate therein day and night, that thou mayest observe to do according to all that is written therein: for then thou shalt make thy way prosperous, and then thou*

shalt have good success. (Joshua 1:8 KJV).

You prospered in all you did because of your spirit of obedience to God and also to Moses.

Many of us struggle to run with someone else's vision. We want everything to originate from us. We want to always be the stars, for the limelight to always shine only on us. As a result we compete unnecessarily when someone else is leading or has been given a word of instruction by the Lord. But you were not like that. You were prepared to run with the vision God had for Israel and your obedience and humility paid off big time.

You accomplished the will of God and to this day, you are an amazing role model not just for your brothers but for the women who continue to admire, respect and appreciate the man you depict, represent and present to us as a Godly example of masculinity, true, Godly masculinity not fake maleness.

Like Christ in John 17:4 you can say:

I have brought you glory on earth
by finishing the work you gave me to do

Refused to be defeated

Many people have given up on things they should either never have started or things they should have fought for. They have packed up on marriages, friendships, their children, dreams, worship and a sound spiritual walk. There are things God has entrusted to each of us which we have not seen to completion like the servant given one talent who buried it (Matthew 25:24). He gave up on it before even trying to see what he could get from it. But this not the sort of man you show us. You refused to accept defeat, you refused to surrender and you fought till every battle was won, and even when Achan caused you to lose a battle (Joshua 7) you got to the bottom of that issue and made sure that all future battles were won. Failure did not exist in your character. You made victory and winning fashionable.

I wonder what the current church would be like, what the body of Christ would be like today if we had the tenacity you displayed. I wonder what marriages and families would be like today if we also refused to lose, refused to be defeated by whatever wiles the devil brought against us. I wonder what our lives would be like if we refused to give up on our dreams, if we kept on singing, kept on writing, kept on submitting proposals and tenders, kept on knocking on doors, kept on praying, tithing and giving.

I pray for that spirit of persistence and consistency that operated in you to also flood the body of Christ again, to saturate marriages and families again and to permeate individual lives so that our dreams become a reality. May we each have that strong spirit which is able to sustain us (Proverbs 18:14) when adversity strikes so that we don't cave in but stand filled with courage and fight on till victory is ours.

These 2 scriptures sum up who you are:

> *Therefore, my beloved brethren, be ye stedfast, know that your labour is not in vain in the Lord. (1 Corinthians 15:58 KJV)*

> *I have glorified thee on the earth: I have finished the work which thou gavest me to do. (John 17:4 KJV)*

Total faith in God

Many of us struggle with trusting God fully, having

the kind of unshaken and unshakable faith you demonstrated as you did what many might consider foolish in circling the city of Jericho fully expecting the walls to fall without canons barraging the walls to weaken them (Joshua 6). You followed God's instructions without wavering and you saw the end of your faith (1 Peter 1:9). How easy it is to profess faith but live in doubt, to profess trust in God but always have a plan B up your sleeve. How many fathers or mothers speak faith as they talk about their children? How many see their children the same way God sees them? How many see their children as the blessed generation of the upright (Psalm 112:2) when their offspring may be behaving like the spawn of the devil?

How many wives trust God to make them the 'good thing' that their husband is supposed to have found (Proverbs 18:22)? Or believe that they can be the Proverbs 31:10-31 woman whose price surpasses rubies? How many have faith that what God said will come to pass even though there may be no outward confirmation? Yet you Joshua demonstrate the type of faith spoken about in Hebrews 11:1:

Now faith is the substance of things hoped for, the evidence of things not seen. (Hebrews 11:1 KJV)

From you we can grasp the confidence-building kind of faith, confidence not in ourselves or our own abilities but confidence in God who is unfailing, whose promises are described in 2 Corinthians 1:20.

Ensuring that others have their inheritance

One of the sad factors about African politics is the fact that when one is in power their focus sometimes excludes the people who voted them into whatever position they occupy. People sometimes do everything they can to line their own pockets to the exclusion of everybody else. This is not an African disease, many times in the western world we see people on trial for stealing or defrauding someone else, not because they are poor but usually because they are greedy. They are selfish and expect everything to belong only to them. They think they live in a vacuum or else they have a warped sense of self-importance where their needs are paramount.

Yet you fought many battles to ensure that it was well with Israel. You were not going to occupy all the land you fought for, you used your position, your skills, your name, your faith to make sure that others possessed their inheritance. That is selflessness, love and true leadership. It is something fathers can learn as they lead their families. It is also something mothers can emulate as they nurture their families. Christ showed us what selfless love is all about, he laid his life down for us, his friends (John 15:13). From him and also from you we learn about selflessly making it happen for others. Celebrating each other, using our money, our names, our positions and every advantage we have to affect and influence someone else's life. You did that as you engaged in battle till all the Israelites had their inheritance, their promised land. Thank you Joshua, role model extraordinaire, lesson learned.

Completing what others leave undone or incomplete

When people take over from others they usually effect change straight away. They want to stamp their individuality on the home, the job, the company and so on. Sometimes the change is a way of fixing what is not broken. In a way we do this as an expression of our pride. We want people to straight away see how much better we are than the other person, we want our style to be immediately evident.

But you were quite happy to complete what Moses started. You took on the same vision Moses had and carried on with it. Yes you heard from God, yes you had a fresh word for what you were doing, but you still used Moses as your reference point and you still ran with the vision he had written and made clear (Habakkuk 2:2). You reminded the children of Israel of what Moses had already spoken to them:

> *Remember the word which Moses the servant of the Lord commanded you, saying, The Lord your God hath given you rest, and hath given you this land. (Joshua 1:13 KJV)*

You didn't rush in with a new word or a new plan, nor did you destroy and trash Moses so that all eyes were on you. Instead you honourably became a steward of the vision entrusted to you. It's never easy to run with another's vision. It takes a special kind of humility and a special kind of strength and wisdom. It means that a person is confident enough of who they are to know that they can serve without losing their individuality or the gifts and talents God has filled them with. They can shine on any platform be it as a waiter, or someone washing cars for others, or as an 'important' CEO of a global corporation.

Thank you for teaching us to be faithful stewards. To be humble enough to run with another man's vision. To be children who can respect their parents enough to obey them and live in their house following and upholding the vision of their parents for their family. From you we learn about order. We learn how even in our homes there are ways things are done that make us family and that eradicate strife and discord. We learn about rank, about following instructions and about the power of agreement (Matthew 18:19).

Thank you for teaching us to be humble enough not to change things simply for the sake of changing them, but to yield not only to the Holy Spirit but to those God has put in authority over us in marriage, family, work, church, nation or any other grouping that we are blessed to a part of.

Thank you also for teaching us that with God nothing is impossible (Luke 1:37), we learn that it is possible to live a truly victorious life, we don't have to accept defeat, and we don't have to be fearful. Challenges are there to be faced and defeated and the more we take them on head on the stronger we become till the enemy knows not to mess with us. We learn from you that God is faithful and that truly his ways are not our ways (Isaiah 55:8). He does not necessarily subscribe to human logic or human methods of defeating foes. God is God and if we know what is good for us, if we want to be victorious then we have to trust him and have faith in him.

I honour and appreciate you and thank you for being such an awesome role-model for today's youth, middle aged folk and the elderly. In fact you are a role- model for anyone who doesn't want to just be a statistic but seeks God's will and wants to do what no one else has done. You are an example of excellence, persistence and victory.

Thank you Joshua.

Love and blessings.

Fari

LETTER 3

HEY BO,

Of all the men in the bible you are probably the one most single women ask God for when they pray. They don't pray for their Adams or their Jacobs or Jobs. When most women pray for a life partner they pray for their Boaz to come, they ask God to bring their Boaz.

I need to get to know you a bit more so that I can understand what it is about you that makes you so attractive. I don't think we are putting you on a pedestal without reason. You are a man that makes people pray to find in a mate what Ruth found in you. Share your life with me, help me understand who you are and why you have become such a great role model and such a Godly example. We find the story of your life in the book of Ruth.

Doing right by someone

It is not easy to do something for somebody without necessarily expecting anything in return. There is usually an expectation of returns on one's investment. People want to know in advance what they will get if they help you out or if they do something for you. But your intention in dealing with Ruth and Naomi seems to have been to be a blessing, to be helpful, to sustain another. When you heard about Naomi's misfortunes, you were willing to help her out. You didn't take advantage of the situation she was in, uou decided to do the honourable thing and went and spoke to the kinsman you felt had more entitlement. Some people would have kept quiet about Ruth and just taken her without doing what was right by her. But you demonstrated honour yet again (Ruth 3:13).

Added to that you made sure her reputation didn't suffer. You made her leave before anyone even saw her and started the rumour mill running. Nowadays we hear of boys totting up what they foolishly refer to as 'conquests'. They count how many virgins they have slept with, they forget that there are laws that we abide by, that seed time is followed at some point by harvest time (Genesis 8:22) and that in some way they will reap the harvest of their sin and their cruelty. But not only did you not touch Ruth, you also protected her honour (Ruth 3:13). Honourable man.

Generous

When Ruth came to glean in your field, picking up what your workers left, you told them to leave more on the ground for her to pick so that in the end she went home with enough food for her and Naomi (Ruth 2:15-16). You didn't need to do this because she was already benefitting from picking up what was left but you were generous and gave her food.

Sometimes we focus so much on what we can get from another we forget that the word says that it is more blessed to give than it is to receive (Acts 20:35). We forget also that it is the generous soul that is refreshed and satisfied (Proverbs 11:25).

Many people determine their ability to give based on how much money they have. They don't realise that there are other ways to give, that time, food, clothing, skills, and strength are all commodities available to us to bless. Poor people remain poor because rather than give from their harvest they write themselves off blessings by expecting to receive always. They don't give of their time or prayers or maybe of the produce from their fields. Someone lied to them and told them that giving can only be done by the rich, by those who have money, and so the rich give and they are blessed, the poor withhold and remain poor (Proverbs 11:24).

One of the things I have made sure I have given even while I had no cash to spare is my time. I have learned not to wait for a full bank account, whatever that is, but rather to give of my time, to open my door to people who may need to come and chill and talk and recharge their batteries. I've realised that I can give my heart and become a mother to the motherless and that does not cost me anything in monetary terms. How blessed it would be if we each gave of our gifts, if teachers taught the excluded kids, if the medical people sacrificed a day a month to help the disadvantages, if the counsellors took time to advise, help and counsel, if the prayerful prayed for those dealing with unimaginable issues. If we each gave of our skills, our time, our prayers and yes our money too. We could indeed make this world a better place for each generation.

So I am excited to notice that you are a generous man, you are a giver and because of it God also ensures that men give to you in good measure, pressed down, shaken together and running over (Luke 6:38). You bring to shame those men and women of influence, people who are in positions of power who make new employees sleep with them so that they can keep their jobs. You expose to the light every selfish act which is done always and only with an expectation of what's in it for the doer.

Appreciative

When you saw Ruth gleaning, one of the things that seemed to touch you was the fact that she wasn't begging but was working. You appreciated her industry and this caused you to speak to your workers so that they made her task easier. You appreciated what she did and even complimented her on it (Ruth 2). I sometimes think that the language of appreciation has been strangled by pride and selfishness and a love of the spotlight. We sometimes fail to realise that light doesn't dim just because it is shining on two people rather than one. I can only imagine how much good we could draw from each other just by showing our appreciation of what a person has done or who they are.

When I used to teach little kids I was always amazed by how far just a little bit of praise went. They would work twice as hard to please someone who was generous with praise and a good word. I know how I feel also when someone comments on something I have done well or something I am wearing. I walk straighter, I am more confident and I try even harder to exceed what that person will have considered to be good. We can all learn the art of appreciation from you Bo, we can all see what our loved ones are doing and take time to speak words of encouragement and create opportunities for them to excel. You did that for Ruth when you asked your workers to leave more grain so that she could pick more and so take more food to Naomi. You appreciated and rewarded her hard work.

From you husbands can learn to appreciate their wives, just as wives could also learn to praise their husbands whenever they do something well. The competitive spirit and the stance of self-preservation currently infiltrating marriages would be quashed. A man can appreciate his wife without losing his masculinity or headship of the home. If she has done something well it makes no sense for a husband to nit-pick and find fault or start lecturing on how things could be done in a better way. People seem to enjoy their 'that's okay but if that was me I would have....' Well it isn't you, it is your husband or wife, they are unique, created in God's image, not yours and so they will do things differently from you, in their own unique way. Appreciate who they are, praise and compliment then on what they achieve and you will coax the best out of them. Praise and appreciation brings the best out of people. Thank you for providing that valuable lesson.

Providing cover

When Ruth under Naomi's tutelage came and slept at your feet, you didn't take advantage of her as some definitely would have (Ruth 3). I'm sure no one would have been bothered, no one would have blamed you, after all she was a widow and a foreigner, both aspects of her life coupled with poverty and desperation made her vulnerable and anyone, you included, could have taken advantage of her under the guise of helping her. But you didn't. Not only did you cover her you also made sure she wasn't compromised and her dignity remained intact.

How many desperate young ladies (and men) have been forced to sleep with selfish and dishonourable bosses for them to be promoted? How many people have abused their positions when they knew that someone was vulnerable because of age, gender or economic status? Yet you remained a man of honour, you did not abuse your position, nor did you take advantage of Ruth's vulnerability. Instead you provided a cover over her. You became a parent to an orphan. You provided education for a poor child, you clothed and fed the widow and covered a naked person's nakedness. You did what Christ exhorts every Christian to do: to feed the hungry, to mourn with those who mourn, to visit those in prison to clothe the naked ... (Matthew 25:36-40).

Thank you sir for the lessons of valour we learn from your life. Thank you for making generosity and genuine kindness fashionable and desirable again. Thank you for quietly presenting yourself as a role model, as a man others can look at learn from and as a leader whose character cannot be questioned.

I remain truly appreciative of who you are.

Blessings always

Fari

LETTER 4

HEY KING D,

King David, I'm afraid you are a bit if an enigma to me. You show both commendable and condemnable traits. Yet your shortcomings reflect your humanity making us realise that just because we fall, fail, or stumble, we don't have to give up or surrender. We also get to put our success in perspective; just because we have been exalted or promoted does not make us immune to the temptations and trials that are 'common to men' (1 Corinthians 10:13; Ecclesiastes 9:3). Despite our human frailty and fragility, we can still end up with favour and a good name with man and more importantly with God (Proverbs 3:4).

As I read about the man you are, I realise that God is more concerned about our motives and our heart than he is with what we do or don't do. If that was not the case I don't think that your name would be esteemed as much as it is. You are that contradiction, that paradox which makes me dig deep within me for a heart that can love and accept people, flaws and all. After all if God could refer to you as the man after his own heart (1 Samuel 13:14; Acts 13:22), and honour some people simply because they are your sons (2 Kings 18:3; 2 Kings 22:2; 2 Chronicles 17:3) regardless of the many mistakes you made, how can I not forgive, not only others but myself also?

I think it is beneficial to explore both your great and not so great moments and attributes. I believe that there are lessons in both and both stamp you as a positive role-model for us even in this day as long as we can see past some of the choices you made or as long as we can learn from them.

Wanting what belongs to another

How many times have we wanted something that belongs to someone else? How many times have we craved, coveted, envied and desired what is not ours? We may not always act on our jealousy or give in to our envy, but none of us can really cast that first stone with a good conscience (John 8:7) in response to what you did regarding Bathsheba, the wife of Uriah (2 Samuel 11). To a lesser or greater extent we have done the same:

- we have been in one place when we know we should be in another
- we have acted on our flesh's desires
- we have tried to hide the products of our actions
- we have destroyed or affected other people's lives
- we have deviously tried to correct the situation with disastrous results

- we have been self-righteous when someone else did something wrong never equating their wrong with ours

There are times in my life when I have tried to wipe the mess I have made but didn't have enough disinfectant, didn't have enough detergent, didn't have a big enough or absorbent enough roll of tissue to get it all clean. I thought I was being clever in cleaning up, but I forgot or acted as if I didn't know that God saw my intent, my action and my reaction. It was all before His all-seeing eyes. You did the same when you tried to correct the mess you had lustfully created. You also seemed to forget that God could see even if people may not have.

There are other lessons for us also encased in your relationship with Bathsheba. One is the fact that sometimes it's not tangible things we crave but destinies and dreams. As parents we sometimes covet what someone else's child is doing and we want it for our own children. In the end there is conflict in the home. We don't express this as covetousness; we camouflage it as parental guidance. But the truth is that we envy the doctor from our neighbour's children and the money he or she will be earning and we wish that could be our own child.

Similarly sometimes we fail to attain our own dreams because we are trying so hard to emulate someone else's dream. We want to sing even though we can't hold a note. We want to lead even though our character is still in need of mending, we want to marry Mr Right even though we don't meet the criteria to be anyone's Mrs Right. We too in many areas of our lives have been chasing things God never intended to be our own. As a result we don't achieve the success we should and we don't attain the dreams we should dream. We become frustrated and covetous of those running in their lane. We trip them up and interfere in their race, not because we are bad people but because we don't have clarity of our own dreams, the grass in the other person's lane appears greener and we want to be over there rather than over here.

We may not have physically killed a man to marry his wife but we may just as guiltily have killed another's dream so that our selfish one could be fulfilled, destroyed another's marriage to fulfil our own lust, tripped another in their lane because we focused on their speed rather than on staying in our own lane or running diligently and consistently our own race.

From the issue with Bathsheba we also learn about having the discernment to be at the right place at the right time, to hear from God so that it can also be said about us that we are daughters of Sarah, doing what is right without fear (1 Peter 3:6). The fact that you were not where you should have been becomes the crux of everything else that proceeded from your unfortunate location. You were lounging on your sunroof when you should have been at war with your men. You were for whatever reason peeping-toming into Uriah's homestead, and you were for whatever reason lonely and idle when as a king I am sure you had the affairs of your nation to attend to (2 Samuel 11). You also decided to act on your despondency and gave in to your lust, leading to a series of unfortunate developments that included adultery, scheming, murder, death, and countless other repercussions of your sitting where you should not have been, of looking where you should not have looked.

Floundering but refusing to stay down

One might assume from what's been said before that we can only learn from the negative things in your life but this is not the case. In fact I wanted to get the negative stuff out of the way so that we can focus on the numerous positive lessons we can all get from the man God loved and referred to as a man after his own heart (1 Samuel 13:14). We can learn from the man who became the yardstick for good kings, the man we all look up to even to this day.

One of the things I most admire about you, by which I have been very encouraged is the fact that you refused to stay down or stay defeated. Regardless of what woes befell you, you seemed to have a spiritual elasticity that got you bouncing back again and again. Sometimes people don't try hard enough at anything. They fail the one time and give up or become too scared to try again. They fail at one relationship and cancel themselves off the dating and marriage scene. They suffer a setback in business and they shut down operations. They lack your mental, and spiritual stamina. They haven't trained their spirit to bounce back or to sustain them in times of adversity and hardship (Proverbs 18:14). As a result, the smallest hurdle destroys them and flattens them. They lack both tenacity and resilience and have mastered the art of complaining to a T.

Thinking about you reminds me of your ancestor Isaac, a man who refused to look at the way things were, who didn't sow only when it rained but carried on sowing even in times of drought and reaped an unusual harvest (Genesis 26:12). He confirms what is said in the book of Proverbs 11:14 that we shouldn't watch the weather but should do right by faith, knowing that God will cause our seed to bring in a sound harvest:

Whoever watches the wind will not plant; whoever looks at the clouds will not reap.

You also bring to remembrance the scripture in Job 22:29 which tells us that our lives don't have to be the same as those of the world, while everyone may be falling and confessing how bad things are, for us there is a definite lifting up. It might be dark and nasty in Egypt but for us in Goshen, in our place in the cleft of the rock, all is well (Exodus 10:23).

This gives me hope, that regardless of how things may appear, regardless of what some may refer to as my 'reality', I can still walk by faith and not by sight (2 Corinthians 5:7). I can sow when I don't have much seed, I can love when I am feeling unloved, I can serve when none serves me and I can be a blessing even while it appears I may not have anything with which to bless. I don't have to wait till I become a millionaire to help someone else, I am blessed to bless even before I see the evidence of that blessing. You teach a good lesson King David. Thank you.

Loving God and serving him as you are

It took me a while to accept that God can use me, work with me and equip me after the mess I made of my life. I struggled to forgive myself and to expect forgiveness from others but most of all to accept forgiveness from him, to know that he could receive me as his own and love me enough to still work in, with and through me. Yet as I read the Psalm you penned and also read your life stories both in the book of Kings and in the Chronicles of the kings, I realise that you refused to allow failure to stagnate your dreams.

Many people stay away from church when things are not going right for them. They either feel too overwhelmed to worship, which is a mistake because worship is a time of answers, it is a time when burdens are removed and it is a time when as we worship in spirit and in truth God comes down and shares that time with us. His word tells us that he inhabits the praises of his people (Psalm 22:3) and I know for a fact that he is not coming down empty handed. His goodness comes with him as does his healing, his strength and power and his love together with everything he is.

Sometimes people also stay away from church because they are ashamed. They have messed up and feel that they can't come to church as if the church pews are full of people who have no issues. That is a lie from hell to stop people from coming to the very place they need to be so that as they continue to hear the word of God they are corrected, they are disciplined they instructed and they are also equipped, provided with the right doctrine (2 Tmothy 3:16) not religious practices and laws that condemn, judge and extradite those who have made mistakes. This is not to say that people should mess up on purpose, the bible is clear on wilful sinning (Hebrews 10:26) and also on what Christ already did so that we don't have to remain in sin (2 Corinthians 5:21).

But from you King David we do learn that nothing can separate us from the love of God which is in Christ Jesus (Romans 8:38-39). He loves us too much to withdraw his grace just because we have erred. He is a loving father who is patient with us and does not deal with us according to our sins (Psalm 103:10). You teach us to come before our father's throne with boldness (Hebrews 4:16) knowing that we are the king's kids, not just any king but The King.

Laying your crown down

In the book of Revelation we read about the elders who took their crowns off to worship the only One worthy of praise (Revelation 4:10). They were important people obviously, hence the crowns, but they knew that their crowns paled into insignificance before their creator. They didn't want their positions and the trappings that accompanied them to hinder their worship, to come between their service and their worship of the one from whom their promotion came (Psalm 75:6).

I have met a lot of people who are so proud of their achievements that they can't talk about anything else but how wonderful they are and how well they have done. They become insensitive to the people around them and become like that proverbial broken record. I think they are surprised to have attained whatever they have that they go on and on about it and cannot talk about anything else. They become name droppers without realising that sometimes other people have achieved even more than they have.

I recall a time when I visited an in-law. A relative of hers was there and she started telling us about snow, showing us pictures of it. She had lived in the UK for some time at a time when the population in diaspora was not large. After she finished educating us on snow, her sister told her that I had lived in the

USA for 4 years. No need to elaborate further. Her pride in her accomplishments as an African who had lived in the UK was so great she could not possibly imagine that anyone else could have done the same or more.

But even though you David were the king of God's people, you didn't hold on to that. In fact you knew that you were only a king because God wanted you to be. You didn't qualify for the post so you couldn't boast about it. You remind me of Christ and how he could come down here and be a human being, and live the life of a human being even though he was and is God. He didn't take advantage of the fact that he was God, he didn't try to use that or focus on that (Philippians 2:6). He was humble and he came and carried all our shame, our pain, our sorrows (Isaiah 53:4). He took every curse that was aimed at us and saw it all nailed to the cross with him (Colossians 2:14). He became cursed so that we through what he took from and for us became free of the curse that was hanging over our lives (Galatians 3:13) in the form of poverty, sickness, failure, oppression and everything else the thief was using to kill, steal and destroy our lives (John 10:10).

You did the same King David. You put aside your crown, your wealth, your qualifications, your status, your kingship and every advantage you had. When you came before the Lord of Lords, you came as David. May I learn from you to set aside whatever special skill, gift, ability or qualification I have and know that when I worship my maker, I set all those things aside and worship him as a child, his child.

Unashamed to worship the King of Kings

Despite your successes as a king and your obvious prowess and strength as a hunter and shepherd, your skill as a composer, poet and leader, you recognised that everything you had and all you were came from something, someone greater than you. You had no allusions of grandeur; you knew perfectly well that your help came from the creator (Psalm 121).

I think sometimes people can be really funny and self-deceiving. We each know who we are, we might deceive other people and yes the heart can be very deceptive (Jeremiah 17:9) but I don't believe that we can deceive ourselves. We know what makes us cry at night when we are alone, we know the things we are capable of doing, we know our shortcomings and we know what we have done even if nobody else may know. Yet sometimes we act all important and perfect as if life starts and ends with us, as if we are indispensable, as if we never do anything wrong. That is when pride seeps in and we can no longer worship God truly. Our supposed importance becomes a hindrance. The blessings become hurdles and we become so important in our own sight that we forget the giver of all good and perfect gifts (James 1:17).

But from you King David I have learned to worship regardless of what may be happening, good or bad. I have learned to analyse my motives when I serve or when I do things for others. I have been reminded, that if I am gifted and talented and I have become better and better at what I do it is not because I am all that, it is because God, my loving father is perfecting that which concerns me (Psalm 138:8). So as I continue to excel and become more and more skilful in my work, it is God that will bring me before kings (Psalm 22:29), he will validate me and bring me to my place of green pastures (Psalm 23). I cannot worship me, I worship him, and that is what you did.

I think that sometimes people face disappointment because they have not put their achievements, skills and gifts in perspective. They have valued their attainments and forgotten the source of them. As a result their worship has been turned inward rather than outward to the one who gave them what they have become so proud of. They have started worshiping the creation rather than the creator (Romans 1:25), but not so you, King David.

So even though I sometimes cringe when I read accounts of your life, I also celebrate when I read the Psalms you penned. You are that paradox of greatness and humanity, of service and selfishness, of worship and some pride, of genuine love for God and self-serving. But as I read about your life, I realise that your position causes your shortcomings to be magnified because of your visibility. Most human beings are complex and contradictory as spirit and flesh vie for eminence. It's just that your contradictions played out on a visible platform whereas most of ours are hidden.

Regardless of what happened in your life, God saw beyond it all to the heart that worshipped the King of Kings. He saw the repentant spirit and the humility of a true worshipper and he made you a role model for us, teaching us that even though we may fall big time, we can still rise up and still be the righteousness of God in Christ (2 Corinthians 5:21).

Thank you King David. One day I hope to sit and listen to you playing your harp. I know that the strings will churn out a love song, loving the one who loved us before we even knew him (1 John 4:19).

Love and blessings

Fari

LETTER 5

HEY PROPHET SAM,

Prophet Samuel I am not quite sure where to begin in talking about you. There are so many lessons we can learn from you and even though you remain one of my favourite prophets, some of the lessons I learn from you are from the mistakes you made or from the times when your

attitude wasn't quite right. But I thank God that you are an encyclopaedia for me, a place from which I can glean wisdom and instruction. God did such awesome things throughout your life from before you were born.

Miracle baby

The things we receive after prayer are so precious. There are a lot of things God does for us without us even asking him to. I know sometimes we forget to acknowledge it but he gives us breath, he keeps our hearts pumping and all the organs and systems, the tissues, cells and every part of us working together, synchronised to keep us alive. He protects us from things we don't even know or see and he showers us with his goodness daily, providing new mercies adequate and exceeding our daily needs (Lamentations 3:22-23). But there are also some things we have prayed for and asked for and it is always exciting to see the responses, the answers and the confirmations of the fact that he hears and answers our prayers.

You are tangible and visible evidence of answered prayer. In fact you became the beginning of repeatedly answered prayers. We read about your mum's prayers and her desire to have a child (1 Samuel 1:10). You came in response to that prayer as God heard and responded to your mother. You have become a reference point for many women who were barren but have looked at you and realised that they too can pray and get answers, they too can implore the Almighty and their wombs like your mother's womb can also be opened. And this does not just refer to physical wombs or uteri, this transcend the physical reaching the financial, spiritual, emotional, relational and social wombs as well.

The miracle you are also gives hope to us all as we pray for other things, and for situations and issues that may not be working right in our lives. If God could hear your mother Hannah, what is to stop him hearing us? If he could respond to her and grant her petition, why would he not do the same for us? Your conception and birth have become powerful precedence of things the God who is the same yesterday, today and forever can and will do (Hebrews 13:8). He is no respecter of persons (Acts 10:34) and we know that what he has done for your mother he will also do in this and every generation for anyone who asks him.

So Prophet Samuel you are a hope stirrer, you are a faith strengthener. By your life story you help us lift our eyes to the hills where we are assured that our help comes from (Psalm 121).

Hearing the voice of the Lord

How hard it must have been for you to be parted from your mother and the rest of your family. How difficult to find yourself living in the temple with an old man and his misbehaving sons (1 Samuel 2:12-17). Yet you seem to have settled down and got on with what needed to be done.

From a young age you heard the voice of the Lord. While so many of our youth are acquainting themselves with the voices of musicians, actors, sports personalities and their peers, you heard the voice of the Lord. When you didn't know that it was the Lord you sought Godly counsel. You asked the one person who could tell you what was happening and clarify the vision for you. You were not too proud to ask and you were not too proud to obey when the instruction came (1 Samuel 3). You were not a young know-it-all who disrespected and brushed aside anyone you considered 'old'. Instead you sought advice and you listened and acted upon that advice.

How many lives could be changed if we all listened to and heard constructive voices as they speak in our lives? How many boys and girls would save themselves a lot of heartache if they allowed their parents to speak into their lives and if they muffled some of the less beneficial voices also trying to speak to them? How fruitful would our lives be if like you we heard God speaking and hastened to obey? How many mistakes could be averted if we sought wise counsel from those qualified by life, anointing, parental role etc to speak to us wisely like the woman described in Proverbs 31 who opens her mouth with wisdom?

Psalm 1:1 (KJV) is a wonderful place to consolidate what we learn from you:

> *Blessed is the man that walketh not in the counsel of the ungodly, nor standeth in the way of sinners, nor sitteth in the seat of the scornful.*

We are blessed if we surround ourselves with wise counsellors, if we make sure that the company we keep moulds us into Godly people. Verse 3 of the same Psalm clarifies the benefits of being wise enough to avoid corruptive company:

> *And he shall be like a tree planted by the rivers of water, that bringeth forth his fruit in his season; his leaf also shall not wither; and whatsoever he doeth shall prosper.*

Our very prosperity be it in marriages, in business, in health, in character etc is reliant on whose voice we listen to and what sort of company we keep. Many are in prison because they kept the wrong company. Many have died of AIDs because they ignored parental counsel and decided to hook up with someone they thought was a hunk. Many are in dire straits because they refused to listen to their parents who told them to take their studies seriously and are now struggling to make ends meet.

As mentioned earlier, you became a role model for current generations before you were born and even as a little boy we can learn from you. For a young boy you exhibited both wisdom and courage and I know that even though she missed you greatly, your mother must have been extremely proud of you.

God's voice

God entrusted you with a lot even while you were a little boy. He spoke to you and told you things about your mentor, his family and their end. He made you a steward of things we assume should have been told to an older and more experienced person. You see we judge people by age, gender, social status and ethnicity while God looks only at the heart (1 Samuel 16:7). We would have searched high and low for a qualified person to carry God's message. We would have dressed them appropriately is colour coded robes relevant to the importance of the news they carry. We would have focussed so much on the trappings and trimmings that in the end the message would pale into insignificance. We would check a person's references and judge them as qualified before we gave them the podium or the pulpit, the stage or the talk show.

But God is not impressed by all that. If need be he will send a child, a donkey (numbers 22:28), a raven (1 Kings 17:4), a widow (1 Kings 17:9) a little boy (John 6:9) and anything and anyone whose heart is right towards him. In fact we hardly ever see him using the self-important and the human-endorsed. He uses the foolish things of the world to confound the wise (1 Corinthians 1:27) and does the unexpected, totally going against the grain.

So you became God's voice and you spoke boldly like Elihu in the book of Job 32:6-9:

> *I am young in years, and you are old; that is why I was fearful, not daring to tell you what I know. I thought, 'Age should speak; advanced years should teach wisdom.' But it is the spirit in a person, the breath of the Almighty, that gives them understanding. It is not only the old who are wise, not only the aged who understand what is right.*

Like Elihu, you refused to allow your youth to be a site of disqualification. You knew that as long as you had the spirit of God leading you, you could stand like David before any foe. You also knew that what you were telling Eli did not originate from you. At that time you probably didn't even have the spiritual vocabulary to verbalise the message you needed to pass on.

What a lesson we can learn. If God has put a word in our mouth, we don't need to prove anything to anyone. That word transcends our qualifications or lack of, it has nothing to do with us, and everything to do with the origin of it. If we realise this, we won't focus so much on the external, on beautifying what people see and on trying to impress. Of course the vessel makes a difference, we need to look good and clean so that we don't drive people away by our scruffiness. But focussing on the external and forgetting the main thing, which is the message can also drive people away as they sense the emptiness, the vanity, the self-centeredness.

If young people knew that God can use them just as mightily as he uses older people, they would take themselves and their lives more seriously. Some of them would begin to attain their dreams and establish secure futures even from an early age. But many play their youth away, they don't realise that there are some things that are not recyclable. Virginity, both male and female cannot be recycled, once it is gone it is gone.

But from you Prophet Sam we learn not to be intimidated by people's age, position, gender, education or origin. We learn to hear from God and act on what he tells us to do regardless of how undercooked and under-qualified we may feel.

Judging by appearance

So many times we give serious credence to our sight, our physical vision. We trust what our eyes tell us and make decisions based on the information they relay back to us. You fell into that trap as well didn't you? You assumed that a king would look, sound and be a certain way. Added to that you assumed that God would choose a king based on how he appeared externally. You thought that the physical attributes translated into excellence within.

We have all done it when we made choices in relationships, churches, jobs, friendship and other important areas of our lives based on how a person or thing looked, how they tickled our senses. We missed out on great friendships because the people didn't fit particular aesthetic specifications. As a result we entered into shallow relationship with people whose spirit we never tested and we paid for it with frustration and sometimes heartbreak.

It amazes me that even though God made us, he is not impressed by our fearful and wonderfully made selves (Psalm 139:14). He knows exactly what went into creating us, he knows the DNA the RNA, the mitochondria, he has a detailed histological and cytological map of each of us and is not in the least bit impressed. I am sure he wonders why some people think melanin is such a big deal. He must wonder why we allow a pigment to determine how we treat each other, whether or not we accept people and whether or not we allow them access to resources and services.

So like many of us have, Prophet Sam you also fell for that trick of the enemy when he focuses on our differences trying to turn them into a site of contention and friction when God intended them to be part of the cacophony of unique beings brought together by their humanity to complement each other as each joint, each skill, talent, language, character supplies what only it can supply to the whole (Ephesians 4:16). Thank God though that he spoke to you and in a few short verses dealt with some 'isms' which we could all learn about even in this day and age. This is what he said in verse 7 of 1 Samuel 16:

> *But the Lord said to Samuel, "Do not consider his appearance or his height, for I have rejected him. The Lord does not look at the things people look at. People look at the outward appearance, but the Lord looks at the heart."*

Proverbs 6:25 adds a bit more meat to the bone that is external appearance:

> *Do not lust in your heart after her beauty or let her captivate you with her eyes.*

Proverbs 31: 30-31 also puts things in perspective by setting physical appearance as unimportant compared to the products of one's industry, the fruit of one's labour and to one's relationship with God:

> *Charm is deceptive, and beauty is fleeting; but a woman who fears the Lord is to be praised. Honor her for all that her hands have done, and let her works bring her praise at the city gate.*

Through these and many other references God helps us to see with more than the physical eye, to assess and work with people seeking and searching for what they are rather than what they look like. We all need that spirit of discernment which allows us to see beyond the physical, the external, the obvious and the visible.

Not pleased with God's choice

I would have thought that after being chided by God in verse 7 that you would have learned your lesson and decided to see things the same way he does. But it appears you had developed a fondness for Saul and you were not too happy with God's rejection of him. I think that was a bit arrogant Prophet Sam. I mean the Creator of the heavens and the earth chooses a king and you sulk because his choice is not what you would have gone for! Maybe I am misunderstanding what happened, maybe you were simply mourning for what could have been. Maybe you were upset because you had seen some potential in Soul but you now realised that he had wasted it. I know there are times when God wants us to let go of certain relationships, habits, people, issues and all that but they are familiar to us, they are part of our past and it is hard to release them even though we know that they are no longer part of God's will for us and for our future.

I suppose you became attached to Saul so it would have been difficult for you to relate to anyone else. But God rejected Saul, and that should have been enough for you to do likewise (I Samuel 15:35; 1

Samuel 16:1). This bring o mind how difficult it was for Abraham to let go of Ishmael even though god told him that he was not part of Abraham's line of blessing. He was a result of human interference and he was Abraham's son. So Abraham struggled to let go even though he knew he should (Genesis 21:11).

Yet I can't be too hard on you. Covetousness rises up in the church sometimes when God chooses people we have condemned. We then envy what they become as God lifts them up. We wonder why he is blessing *them* considering their litany of sins. We judge people and find them lacking based on whatever scale we have weighed them on. We write off some people because of their past and like you we sulk when God decides to use those flawed and unqualified people to do his work. The sulk sometimes is just an external manifestation of our pride. We are hurt because God hasn't called for a meeting to discuss with us and consult us on the person to appoint for this or that post, the person to anoint for this or that ministry. We think so highly of ourselves, more highly than we ought to (Romans 12:3) to the point where we have appointed ourselves as advisers for Yahweh, hence the sulking.

But we need to learn, like you had to that God looks at the heart. He considers the motives more than the well -set hair, or the 3-piece suit, or the long prayers or all the religious traditions and gimmicks. God is not going to change his mind to fit in with our jaundiced and prejudiced view of people. When he has made his choice, we should celebrate it and move on.

As a father: didn't learn from Eli

What I will say now may sound harsh Prophet Samuel but then remember I did say earlier that I have learned not only from your positive attributes but also from some of your shortcomings. The aspect of your life that baffles me the most is how your children turned out. That is an issue I still cannot fully grasp.

Prophet Samuel you were the mouthpiece used by God to bring judgement on Eli and on his sons (1 Samuel 3:11-14). As a child you heard from God and you were a faithful steward of the message he gave you. Yet when I look at your own children, they were not much better than Eli's and that is what baffles me. You knew how God felt about Eli's spoilt brats of sons. You knew how angry God was with Eli's permissive parenting. Yet you seem to have walked in exactly the same path he did. What was that all about?

> *When Samuel grew old, he appointed his sons as Israel's leaders. The name of his firstborn was Joel and the name of his second was Abijah, and they served at Beersheba. But his sons did not follow his ways. They turned*

aside after dishonest gain and accepted bribes and perverted justice (1 Samuel 8:1-4).

I think parents sometimes forget who they are or who they are supposed to be in their children's lives. Some parents are the children and their children become the parents dictating and deciding what is done and not done in the family. Unfortunately parents seem to be slow to realise that they are grooming and nurturing criminal tendencies in their children. They don't realise that when little Mafta keeps hitting other children and nobody intervenes he he then graduates to more serious things. He can then start hurting other children because those who should be training him the way he should go (Proverbs 22:6) have moulded his behaviour by their silence.

Failure to correct is just as damaging instilling wrong values whether it is through parental silence or through teaching the wrong thing. Sometimes people forget that their children are theirs and that not everyone will treat them like princes and princesses. You can't make people love your kids or want to spend time with them more so if they are spoilt brats. There are children you just don't want to visit not because they are bad but because mum and dad are so permissive that you know having the children will not be the joy it should be.

Having seen Eli's children in action, you should have studied them and seen where they went wrong so that you could spot problems in your own kids and discipline them accordingly. This is not to say that parents are to blame when their children go crazy. No, each person is an individual who has free will and sometimes it doesn't matter what parents do, some kids still mess up. But if as a parent you know that you have instilled the right values, you have corrected and loved and done your best, you are not responsible for the choices your kids make as adults. They have the power to make their own decisions, but the radar you secured in them remains and as parents we all then pray that it directs them back to:

......whatever is true, whatever is noble, whatever is right, whatever is pure, whatever is lovely, whatever is admirable--if anything is excellent or praiseworthy.... Philippians 4:8

So thank you Prophet Sam, your life has provided some sobering lessons for me. It has made me rethink how I view people, who I am as a parent and how I serve in my Father's house. Having said all I have said though, I am glad it is not my life that is written down in so much detail for the world to read and even judge. I wonder what people would learn from me, or how harshly they would judge me for my times of failure. So for that reason I cannot be too hard on you because regardless of what you went through, what mistakes you made, and what areas you appear to have failed in, I can still say that you are an awesome role model.

Thanks Prophet Sam

Blessings always

Fari

LETTER 6

Hi G,

Gideon many people preach about you, many use your life as an illustration of both fear and strength, of doubt and faith, of God's favour and human scepticism. You provide an excellent parallel between what is Godly and what is human. I think your life is an excellent one to explore and study; it is a life that can bring hope to people who struggle with a sense of despair, inferiority and fear.

Unaware of who God says you are

One of the blessings God has showered me with over the last few years is an increasing awareness and knowledge of who I am. Colonialism did a great job of filling me with a sense of inferiority, a hopeless sense of never qualifying and not being good enough.

Migrating from Africa initially to USA to study then the UK to live both reinforced the sense of my life being out of control, of some people qualifying for what I could only dream about, not because they were better than me or more academically qualified, but a lot of the time because they were lighter in complexion than me.

I know it may not be politically correct to openly address these issues because they make some people uncomfortable. But my task is not to make anyone comfortable. It is to speak healing through scraping off the false scab that hides festering sores, then apply the healing balm of the word on the wound so that it can heal properly and with finality.

So being in the UK and having to continually respond to stupid questions about my difference really did not do much for my already floundering self-esteem. But this is where the genuine and tangible goodness of God set in and was revealed to me till it got to the point where it overwhelmed me. He finally got it through my stumbling self that I am not an accident. I am different because he wanted me to be different and made me so. I am absolutely fantastic in the vessel he has shaped me in and I don't need to justify my presence to anyone, I don't need to second guess myself and I certainly should not allow anybody to make me feel as if I am not worthy of the blessings that are due me.

Unfortunately it is not only the secular world that highlights difference and erects social ladders. There are some places of worship where people are given positions not based on anointing or God's appointment but because of how they look. There are places of worship where the 'us' and 'them' culture is perpetuated by religious traditions where Galatians 3 and verse 28 in particular are not known. It took me a while to find a church where I could offload the massive chip that was on my shoulders. There were places I went to where many had the chip raised high and where they did not receive their 'word in season' 9Isaiah 50:4; Proverbs 15:23). But when God brought me to the brook where he allowed my feet to find rest, the Rock that is my Lord and Saviour crushed that chip to a pulp.

So Gideon I can identify with what you were going through. I don't condone it or agree with it but I can identify with it because I also had to be worked on my the word, in fact the word had to do some serious convincing to get me to a place where I could look in the mirror and see a beautiful woman. I read this excerpt of Song of Solomon 1 and it speaks to me, maybe differently than the way it would speak to another, but it talks to me:

> *Dark am I, yet lovely, daughters of Jerusalem, dark like the tents of Kedar, like the tent curtains of Solomon..*
>
> *Do not stare at me because I am dark, because I am darkened by the sun.*

My mother's sons were angry with me and made me take care of the vineyards; my own vineyard I had to neglect.

Tell me, you whom I love, where you graze your flock and where you rest your sheep at midday. Why should I be like a veiled woman beside the flocks of your friends?

Gideon I am not going to try and discuss the verses above. I have highlighted the bits that really talk to me. I will leave them italicised so that they can also speak to others. But one thing I can tell you for sure is that stares don't faze me, I will no longer delegate my dreams to the shelves while I am making everybody else's dreams come true, and there will not be a veil over my face. God has already confirmed this to me through Isaiah 49 that I am for the display of his splendour so I am not going to be hidden away anymore. I know who I am and I know whose I am and right now I am just waiting for my father to put the finishing touches to the awesome table he is preparing for me in the presence of whatever has been an enemy to me (Psalm 23).

Called, unaware of what is in you

This is what was said to you:

> *The Lord turned to him and said, "Go in the strength you have and save Israel out of Midian's hand. Am I not sending you?"* (Judges 6:14)

How hard it must have been to hear those words while you were still in a place of confusion, in a place where things didn't add up or sit right. You were in a winepress but you were threshing wheat (Judges 6:11). I believe inside you knew you were better than what you were seeing but the reality of what was around you did not agree with the vision within or with what God was saying to you. Unlike others you didn't just hide away and do nothing. Even at a time when your faith was little, yet you remained resourceful and proactive. You didn't allow the enemy to ride roughshod over you. So even though it appeared as if things were out of control, you took action and found a way to do something to save your family by rescuing some food from the enemy, by outsmarting the enemy, showing that you were a step ahead.

Isaiah 49:1 is an awesome scripture. It's one of the verses God has used to get me to see with clarity, to realise that I am something special. It's sad to realise that the material that creates greatness is already in us but we are unaware of it, just like you were unaware that you were already called to be a leader, called to deliver your people. God has done what needs to be done but until we take time to find out what is in us; we can live in ineffectiveness, in lack and poverty, in sickness. We can be in hiding like your people were, hiding in caves and mountain clefts (Judges 6:2) when a deliverer is in our midst already.

The bible tells us that it is from the fullness of the heart that the mouth speaks (Matthew 12:34). Our speech reflects what is in us, the depth of our insecurity or strength. The Lord was speaking to you but in reflection to what was within you, what was in your heart, you started spewing off about your lineage as if God didn't already know which tribe and which family you emanated from. Then you had to go and 'if' God in verse 17 and 36! Doubter language in the face of the Almighty God!

I know there are times when I have disqualified myself because of my past, my marital status, my complexion, my ethnicity or my age among other factors. I have chosen to look at my circumstances instead of looking to the hills from where my help comes (Psalm 121). But when I look at what you accomplished as recorded in Judges 7, then I know we serve a merciful, patient and kind God. I know regardless of the mess of the past, my future is bright, it is assured and his plans for me as they were for you are for good and not evil and they will bring me to my place of hope, a future and an expected end (Jeremiah 29:11).

Mighty man of valour

After all is said and done Gideon, you are a mighty man of valour. You are a man whose life can be an inspiration to those who may have been in constrictive circumstances which also appeared hopeless. As they relate with you, they can also learn that the intrinsic value and worth of man is not determined by place of birth, country of origin, melanin levels, education and other socially determined qualifications. A man's value is put in him by the God who created him and breathed both life and Godliness into him.

It is funny how people try to disqualify each other. When I read the bible in Genesis 1 the only demarcation or distinction God made was in relation to gender. He made them male and female. He doesn't say that he made them black and white, rich and poor, educated and uneducated. He made them male and female. So where all the rest of the stratification comes from is a mystery. Why we decide to emphasise and stress what God did not instruct us to is a mystery.

In getting to know you I realise that I am pre-packed with excellence. Even though they may not have realised it, my parents were presented with a bundle of joy infused with gifts and skills and an awesome destiny. They didn't realise what a gold mine they had in their hands. But I thank God for his grace so that even though I was slow in realising who I am, I have realised it. I am not going to be like so many people who die never having known who God made them to be, what God gifted them with, and what destiny God mapped out for them. Just like you finally realised that you are a mighty man of valour, I am also realising that I am woman whose prize exceeds rubies (Proverbs 31:10) and that I am beloved and precious in God's eyes (Isaiah 43:4). I am destiny-changer, a trail-blazer, an encourager of those people who feel like they have reached the end of the road and a conduit not only of God's love but of blessings that change and transform lives (Genesis 12:3; Acts 3:25; Genesis 28:14).

Focussing on human identity

I think that most people struggle to marry their identity based on God's word and their identity that family, society and the voice within has dictated. You were no different as evidenced by your incredulity when you heard what God was saying to you in Judges 6. Your responses indicate a man who didn't agree with what was said to and about him.

You are not the first person to feel like that. Many of us have also had the quiet debates reflecting the turmoil between our perceptions of who we are and what the word of God says. We assume that we are not as good as God says we are. Sometimes we fight against God's word and are surprised when people see something great in us because we have not yet seen it.

There are many great people who had to deal with the issue of identity. They too had to weigh their own perceptions of themselves against God's word and they had to concur with Elisha when he told his servant in 2 Kings 6: 15-16 that they were not insignificant and vulnerable but that they were part of a great army. We also need to know that we are powerful people, not in and of ourselves but because we are God's children and he has made all grace abound towards us and he has made sure that we are fully equipped for whatever it is we need to do (2 Corinthians 9:8).

Both Abraham and Sarah his wife had to line up their thinking with God's. They were both so focussed on their humanity that they actually both laughed when they were told about their productive future (Genesis 18:12; Genesis 17:17) I know we hear a lot about Sarah's laughter but in reality both husband and wife didn't believe that they could be parents just like someone right now cannot believe they can be called to become a preacher, or a doctor, or a Godly parent, or a blessing. The natural manifestation of themselves outweighs the Godly reality. So you are not the only mighty man of valour who didn't know that he was mighty or that there was any valour in him. But I'm glad you did eventually agree with who God said you were and you went out in your strength and saved your people, God's people (Judges 7).

My prayer is that we would silence the human declarations of who we are and hear what the word of God says, believe what God is saying. Because we are sometimes too close to the issues, challenges and situations we live through, we cannot always see clearly. Our proximity to our situations causes us to see things in blown out, out of proportion bits. The logs in our eyes (Matthew 7:5; Luke 6:42) block our view and we end up with a totally distorted view not only of who we are but also of what we are going through. This is why it is important to view ourselves as God views us and to allow his thoughts to infuse our thoughts since we know that his thoughts and plans for us are for good always and never for evil and that he intends for us to have a hope and a future (Jeremiah 29:11).

It's crucial to also know that his ways are higher than ours (Isaiah 55:9). We see ourselves imperfectly but his ways are higher than us and he sees us from a view that is inclusive of all detail, a view that has the right perspective. His omnipotence allows God to see the beginning, middle and end of each issue and to know the intricate details we may not know because of our human limitations and our inability to always see as God sees. As a result, his opinion is always better, his thoughts always better, his definition of who we are and what we can do always better.

So I am glad G that you eventually did see what God saw and you eventually accepted what God said about you and you eventually stopped testing not only God's sincerity but also his authenticity. You finally realised that you are indeed a mighty man of valour, and once you acknowledged that, you didn't need to remain in hiding or continue to use trickery, and secrecy. You were released by the truth you now knew (John 8:32) and you became the man God had always said that you were.

How wonderful if each child of God stopped arguing with God, stopped testing him and started instead to run in the lane God points out, doing exploit in their own area of gifting and stepping out in confidence to fulfil their individual and corporate destiny.

Regardless of how long it took you to be the man you were destined to be, I am glad that you did become him. Many people die unfulfilled never having realised that they are wired for great destinies. But you present a precedent for us that indeed to the living there is hope (Ecclesiastes 9:4) that indeed just because we mess up or fail we can still get up and run (Micah 7:8; Proverbs 24:16). For that I thank you.

Doubting and questioning God's word

God uses people, angels, his word and many other avenues including that 'still small voice' (Isaiah 30:21; 1 Kings 19:12) to reassure us and to let us know who we are. He knows our insecurities and has found so many different ways to let us know how precious we are, how much he loves us. Unfortunately despite all these ways he has put in place sometimes we still doubt and question and we even set challenges for him. We want the Holy one of Israel (Isaiah 12:6; Isaiah 43:3; Isaiah 54:5) to prove that he can do what he says he will do so we let him qualify the only way we know how to show or earn a qualification. We let him sit a test!

Gideon in Judges 6:36-40 you approach God with an expression of doubt, you go to him using the 'if' word. You put Jehovah through the hoops. When he 'passed' the first test you gave him a second one. Numbers 23:19 should be enough for us all, the knowledge that God is faithful to his word and the fact that he can do what he says he will do. He is not like man who promises in all good intentions but cannot always deliver.

So there is no need to give God practical or written tests so that he proves to us that he will or can do what he promised. We have to be convinced within ourselves of his love and of his willingness and ability to make things happen for us. After all he is the giver of all good gifts (James 1:17).

In addition to putting God to the test, we also seem to want to force ourselves to be part of the solution. When the word talks about healing, telling us that we are healed already by his stripes (Isaiah 53), we still consider the 'obvious' things: how long we have been ill, how bad the prognosis is, how we feel, what our friends and those who have had similar symptoms say, what the internet says, how unrealistic the promise of health and healing is. We have to be part of the solution.

Our age (or financial situation, gender, origin, ethnicity etc) has to qualify us otherwise we cannot accept what we are being promised:

- Sarai and Abram both laughed at the ridiculous promise that they could in their old age become parents to Isaac, the child of promise (Genesis 18:12; Genesis 17:17)

- Mary considered her virgin state and asked how she could have a child without the natural process of copulation (Luke 1:34)

- Zechariah found it hard to believe that he and Elizabeth could in their old age become parents to John the Baptist (Luke 1:18)

- Jesse and Samuel both assumed God would choose one of the older and more appropriate Kingship candidates. Neither thought that God would choose David (1 Samuel 16).

- King Saul also tried to add his birth, his tribe, his family into the equation of qualification (1 Samuel 9:21).

- You also started talking about your clan and that you were the least in your family. You seemed to think that God didn't know you that maybe he appointed you by mistake (Judges 6:15).

All the above could have learned a good lesson on perspective from the Apostle Paul (1 Corinthians 15:9). He knew that his calling as an apostle had nothing to do with him but everything to do with God and his grace. Paul did not try to present God with a CV. He knew that God is the one who promotes (Psalm 75:6) not qualifications, not birth, not genealogy, not country of origin.

I don't know if this fixation with ourselves is a weird form of humility or if it a sense of superiority when the natural is always regarded as being the main consideration. I know that in many cultures and in many religions you are not supposed to sell yourself, in fact you are supposed to underplay your ability or achievements so that you don't appear pompous. Your confessions have to also show how humble you are; you can't acknowledge your own skills, your prowess in any field or just how awesome you are. It appears this 'humility' is a commendable trait. But that kind of humility to my thinking, in my opinion is a weapon successfully used by the devil to stop believers and non-believers from realising the power of their words, their self-perception and their view of themselves. It stops us acknowledging and speaking God's word into our own realities.

The word of God tells us who we are in Christ and that is the view we should have of ourselves. We need to have our thinking renewed (Romans 12:1) not by current pedagogical trends but by the word of God and by the Holy Spirit.

It is no longer time to accept things just because they have been passed down the generations, a cut-off point is needed; the buck has to stop here. What God says is what we should expect and accept not what society dictates. It is high time we knew who we are in Christ and it is high time we accepted his definition of us. There is no need to buy into the world's false humility. As he is so are we in this world (1 John 4:17) and we are the righteousness of God in Christ (2 Corinthians 5:21) we are not sinners saved by grace, we used to be sinners but are no longer defined by our sinful past.

Reality vs God's word

Some people consider themselves to be 'realists'. I am assuming this means that they see things as they are, as they really are. They believe in what they see not what is supposedly out there. These tend to be 'practical' people who want to 'see' things and who don't believe in anything they cannot confirm or connect to via their senses. But faith is the substance of things hoped for (Hebrews 11:1), these things may not be in evidence to the sensual side of us, but this apparent invisibility does not negate their reality. The same faith is also defined as the evidence of things that are not seen, things that have not been manifested to the sensual world. Yet we are being told that there is evidence of these things presence regardless of whether or not our human senses can grasp, perceive, imagine or acknowledge them.

Like most of us G you also got into that difficult time of trying to marry what you perceived as real and the unimaginable that was being presented to you. You struggled with the two opposing concepts of there being 'evidence' of things you couldn't see and the 'believe what you see' logic instilled in you probably by your parents but also by the environment that nurtured you and the issues you faced each day which did not present much hope to you.

A person who was abused as a child may regard that abuse as their reality. They may expect their life to continue in the pain, despair and fear instilled by their lived experiences. They would struggle to accept the love that is genuinely and freely offered not only by God who is love (1 John 4: 7-8) but also by people around them. Their pain may continue to stamp a reality for them that makes it difficult for them to believe in the yet unseen, in the possibility of their living happy lives, in the possibility of them marrying well and becoming loving parents.

I don't believe that there is a unit called reality. I believe that real reality is a conglomeration of seen and unseen, tangible and intangible, obvious and incredible, normal and abnormal things which if permitted all shape our destiny. The visible reality of our lived experiences should not be accorded superiority over the things we may not see, know or understand as yet which never-the-less are just as significant an aspect of our identity. The pain of a wound should not negate the work which though invisible is already being done by platelets, the immune system and the apparently invisible hand of God. The arrival of unending streams of bills is no more our reality if we are children of God than the reality of his supply and provision which he has promised (Philippians 4:19) and since we know he does not lie (Numbers 23:19), we therefore know that it is already happening.

Sarah, Rebekkah, Hannah, and Rachel's barrenness appeared to be their reality but we all know that they became mothers.

Our task is to refuse to let what seems to appear to have precedence over what may not as yet appear. We have to deny eminence to what we see over what seems to be invisible. Our eyes should not have the power to dictate our future over our faith and our trust in God. What God says about us should reign over what we feel, see, hear, taste, smell or even believe. His word which is settled in heaven (Psalm 119:89) should guide what we accept and what we expect for our lives.

In conclusion G let me encourage someone who didn't know they were mighty to go out in their might and save their family, let that virtuous woman who wasn't aware of her virtue go and do exploits and show that she is a daughter of Sarah who does what is right without fear (1 Peter 3:6). Let that sick person go out knowing that the sun of righteousness has risen over them with healing in its wings (Malachi 4:2). Let that weak person declare and believe that they are strong (Joel 3:10).

Thank you for the lessons you have provided, for being an excellent role model who didn't pretend to have it all together but who in the end conceded to the higher authority, the more sure word of prophecy (2 Peter 1:19) which drew out the might that was already within you.

Love and blessings

Fari

LETTER 7

Hey CAL,

It's such a pleasure to think about you and to put my thoughts down. You are a man of such dignity and soundness of character. What a blessing for Moses to have had you and Joshua, men that could be trusted, men of few words who were not gossipers or stirrers of strife.

People used to reprove women for gossiping but the generation I live in seems to have turned things round. Men are now bigger gossipers, talebearers and whingers that a lot of the women in their lives. They grumble and murmur and can't seem to stop talking! Obviously not all men are like that but there seems to be an increasing number who haven't realised that there is dignity in silence, in truth and in not being busybodies.

I can just imagine how many pastors and other leaders would gladly have you in their team, leading and ministering with a sincere heart and with a genuine attitude to serve.

Maintained strength

Many people disqualify themselves when they get to a certain age. They stop dressing well or generally taking care of their physical appearance. They allow themselves to retire from life and assume that they have reached the end of the road. They stop planning, they stop dreaming, they stop contributing and assume they have nothing worthwhile to give to their society and their generation. Sometimes this is not because that is how they feel within themselves but more a case of how they are made to feel by their children and their society.

Society tends to vilify age, and to marginalise those who have reached a particular age. Visible disciplines like Television work hire younger and firmer-bodied individuals over more mature candidates and older people are gradually relegated to background work where supposedly people can't be offended by their grey hair or their wrinkles. This harshness seems to be directed more at women than men because there are a lot of grey-haired male presenters but not that many females.

But when I read your life story, you seem to have refused to bow to societal pressures to retire and you maintained your strength so that even at 85 you were a force to reckon with. You denied age-defined expectations. You were obviously not a sloppy man who ate anything and everything; you were not neglectful of your health. I don't think you had a fat-tire around your waistline and I don't think you would have gone out of breathe by just climbing the stairs. You seem to have held on to the fact that your body is a temple of the Holy Spirit (1 Corinthians 6:19). How else could you have said the following statement at 85? How could said statement not just be boasting but your reality?

> *[11] I am still as strong today as I was in the day that Moses sent me; my strength now is as my strength was then, for war and for going and coming. [12] So now give me this hill country of which the LORD spoke on that day….. (Joshua 14:11-12a)*

Accomplishments and success are not only for the young. It would be lovely to attain our goals in our youth but the reality for most people is that life presents some unanticipated detours and we don't always reach our destiny at 20 or even at 40. For some of us, we only realise our purpose when we hit 50 either because we were too foolish to see or we allowed too many voices to speak in our lives, causing an advice traffic jam that hindered our progress and delayed our arrival. Some people had the misfortune to have hurdles and blockades thrown in their path by circumstances they could not sail over at that time. As a result, they couldn't make the progress they wanted to. Whatever the reason, many people begin to see clearly later in life. That being the case, they cannot afford to give up just because they are older. They still need to run with their vision and like you not allow the enemy's delaying tactics to succeed.

Moses had confidence in you

When Moses selected twelve spies you were among them representing the tribe of Judah (Numbers 13:6). He must have prayed for direction and guidance and maybe he consulted the tribes before making his final selection of twelve. He must have been sure that he had made the right choice and that the interests of each tribe would be well-represented.

Moses sent you, Joshua and the other 10 on an important assignment. The man of God got two out of twelve right. His confidence was misplaced in ten cases and only spot-on in two. It happens sometimes that you entrust a job to someone thinking that they will do it well only to find out later that you misplaced your trust and your confidence; you gave the job or your love to the wrong person. But I thank God you were the man for the job, you and Joshua were a perfect choice and Moses had no regrets in having chosen and sent you.

I wonder how God feels about the assignments he has sent us on. I wonder if we are able to return always like you Caleb and Joshua and give a truthful and honest report or if we embellish the truth so that we look good before our leaders. Maybe our reports don't explain in detail in case we are then sent back to deal with the giants we saw in the land we spied. Or maybe we allow our own failures and inadequacies to judge situations instead of looking at issues with hope and trust and an attitude of faith.

Paul was confident of Timothy, as a result he could openly instruct him confident of Timothy's character and confident of what was in him, the fullness of his heart from which he would speak (Luke 6:45; Matthew 12:34). Paul also expressed similar confidence in Onesimus in Philemon 1:11 sending him to Philemon knowing that he was useful. Moses must have had similar confidence in the 12 men he selected to send out as spies, unfortunately his confidence was misplaced.

Sometimes people in leadership promote certain people because they talk right or look right. They don't get to know who these people are and as a result they mess up on the job. Some are too proud to be led, wanting to be leaders even though they are not ready, wanting to be seen even though they have no content and no depth. They then mess up on the job.

Leaders don't always get to know the people they lead because people put their best foot forward for them. They are intent on pleasing in order to be promoted and in the end they are fake. Some spend time talking about other people as a way of securing their own position. Unfortunately not all leaders have the wisdom and discernment to see that they are surrounded by false reporters, by insecure gossipers who destroy anyone who tries to rise. They lose good people whose efforts to serve are frustrated by the inner circle. Sad to say even in churches, pastors are sometimes surrounded by people who find a way to get close then turn around and bob down anyone who also tries to gain access to the servant of God.

How wonderful it would be if the majority rather than the minority of people who are close to leaders had your character, if their 'nay' could really be 'nay' and their 'yes' be 'yes' (James 5:12). The sheep would be safer if leaders had genuine shepherds around them, bringing truthful reports like you and Joshua did.

Numbers 14:24 different spirit

In these times where conformity seems to be the norm, I am glad that there is a man like you for our sons to look up to and for all of us to emulate.

We serve a God of order and peace (1 Corinthians 14:33) but I also know that we serve a God who made each of us wonderfully and fearfully (Psalm 139:14), he made us uniquely and infused into each of us what we need to fulfil our own destinies. Just looking at an array of faces on the bus or on a plane or even in the street should make us see how much God; our creator values our uniqueness and our individuality. He never meant for us to imitate others or to try to be replicas and copy cats. To each of us he gave intelligence, the ability to reason out things, to think and assess. But there are lot of brain-lazy people out there who can't be bothered to think things through. Instead they just accept what the majority says and they become crowd-pleasers.

But you and Joshua obviously cannot be included in that paint-brush description of your peers. You went to spy the land and you did not try to agree with everyone's assessment. The honour within you did not allow you to parrot back to Moses what everyone else said. Instead the spirit of truth in you had you speaking what you saw and giving an assessment that was not laced by fear and intimidation. You had a different spirit, a spirit of truth, boldness and honesty. You didn't try to mesh with the crowd and be like everyone else. You were willing to stand alone and stand for the truth.

A lot of trouble that young men and women get into is because they are desperate to be part of what they think is the in-crowd. They go through horrendous and sometimes embarrassing initiations to become part of fraternities and sororities and they turn against their parents because the new crowd is more fashionable. Some sacrifice their beliefs and the teachings their parents have instilled in them just so that they can be accepted. They don't realise that some of the groups they so desperately want to belong to are led by some weakling feeding off their desperation to belong. They become devious, and lie and rebel just so that they can belong.

There are even grown men and women who don't make decisions in their homes without consulting 'friends'. They don't have confidence in their own intelligence and wisdom; they don't trust God enough to consult *him* rather than their colleagues.

So they end up receiving multiple and conflicting counsel and in the end they do not make any progress. They don't realise that their advisers also have their own agenda and not all is beneficial to them.

You may ask how I know this and the answer is simple. I was in a whirlwind of people-pleasing for a long time, as a result I remained in one place trying to work out the conflicting advice I was receiving from friends and from family. It took me settling in a church where the word was taught so that in all my getting I started to get some understanding (Proverbs 4:7) and finally realised that God has already equipped me with all the gifts and material I need to succeed. Instead of asking *him*, the author and perfecter of my faith (Hebrews 12:2) the giver of all good and perfect gifts (James 1:17) the shepherd who leads me in still waters (Psalm 23), I was asking people, listening to people, acting on people's advice. This is not to say that one mustn't listen to advice, the bible tells us that with many advisers our plans succeed (Proverbs 15:22). But you have to be selective in who you allow to speak into your life and I wasn't.

But Caleb I thank God that you show and demonstrate that there is honour in being a man of your word. There is honour and God rewards truth and integrity. You teach character, that a man should be able to speak truth even from a minority platform, even if no one else is speaking truthfully, even if he is on the outside shouting in. You make me realise that my focus should not be on merging or blending but on being true to the woman God wants me to be not who society says I should be.

Thank you for showing that there is nothing wrong with being different, with not wanting to be part of the gossip mill, with not wanting to be popular at the expense of being honourable.

Territory taker

I think one of the lies of the enemy that has continued to affect people over generations is fear to be the first. This need to walk on tarred roads, this need to follow and be led had hindered and minimised many lives. People even discourage you doing things if no one else has done them in the family. Teachers' children are encouraged to carry on the 'family tradition' even if the family has suffered financial hardship because of the poor pay the parents got. People seem to like the tried and tested. Not you.

It's hard being the first in any area because there is no precedence; there is no plan to build from, no smooth road to cruise on. Being a pioneer and a territory taker requires stamina and it requires an unnatural determination to succeed at all odds. Unfortunately not everyone has the will or inclination to go beyond the ordinary and the bare minimum. But you did.

Strange enough though, envy reigns when someone decides to clear the forest and build on their dreams. Our society and our generation has turned fame and wealth into instant coffee look-alikes. Everyone thinks they can just turn up somewhere and become rich and famous. As a result people go to untold extents to get that contract, nail that gig, get into that circle. They want the result without the process.

Not fearful or intimidated by how things appear

You really are an awesome role model Caleb. When you make a decision you don't allow the way things appear to hinder you or to side-track you. You go for what needs to be done. You are not fearful, you are not intimidated, and you do what needs to be done even if no one else has ever done it.

When you presented your report to Moses you didn't need to consult with your peers and doctor up the report to make it politically correct and acceptable. You reported what you saw as you saw it:

> *I was forty years old when Moses the servant of the LORD sent me from Kadesh Barnea to explore the land. And I brought him back a report **according to my convictions*** Joshua 14:7

You reported according to your convictions not according to what was popular or what was acceptable. You reported the truth without embellishing it or creating hype around it.

I remember being invited to a beautiful house. As I entered I felt like taking my shoes off. It was so beautiful I started to feel intimidated. Already I was disqualifying myself feeling like the grasshoppers described by the ten spies in Numbers 13:3:

We saw the Nephilim there (the descendants of Anak come from the Nephilim). We seemed like grasshoppers in our own eyes, and we looked the same to them

I felt like a grasshopper in my own sight even though this family was welcoming me into their home with love. I was overwhelmed by the size and beauty of the home and I listened to the wrong voice which affected how I felt.

But you went into the awesome set-aside land, God's inheritance for his children and you acknowledged the beauty, the wealth, the prospects, the challenges and every aspect of that land. Yet you were not frightened, you were not intimidated. You knew that God had not given you a spirit of fear but of love and of power and of a sound mind (2 Timothy 1:7). You knew that God wanted you to see what he saw in the land because he didn't describe the giants but rather that the land was good (Genesis 17:8; Leviticus 20:24).

People don't always take time to analyse the reasons for their inaction and their acceptance of less than enough, less than their best. Fear is irrational. It is a wasteful emotion draining you of energy that should be directed towards solutions. Fear cripples and binds you paralysing you and hampering your progress. Sometimes it becomes part of people daily language as they make statements like' 'I'm afraid I can't make it'. It's a perfectly innocuous statement but at the same time it introduces and welcomes an enemy into one's speech and attitude. Fear is evil, it is not Godly.

Think about how abusive people keep their victims in line. They fill them with fear of what will happen. They fill them with fear of a future without the abuser. They play on their insecurities and coerce them into silence using various threats. Fear is a force, a negative force and it is not part of our identity, not part of who we are in Christ. Thank you for demonstrating fearlessness and courage.

Not afraid of hard work

I think many of us could learn from you. You were a man who at 85 years of age was prepared to not only receive your land but you were prepared to even tackle mountains; the huge challenges that face most people, the hurdles, the hardships, the family situations, the marital and financial issues. In today's language you would be saying 'Bring it on!' (Joshua 7:10-14).

I come from a line of industrious women. My maternal grandmother was well known for industry. As kids we didn't really like visiting her during the rainy season or harvest time when there was a lot of work in the fields. She worked hard and this meant that we also had to spend hours in the field alongside her. When she wasn't in the field she was crocheting doilies which earned her a nickname. She travelled even in her 80s to neighbouring countries selling her doilies and purchasing stuff she needed for her home. She never seemed to sit still but then neither did she ever lack.

My mother also followed in her mother's footsteps. She could coax vegetables and flowers to grow even in the stoniest of ground. She cared for her husband and home, she knitted, she sewed, she raised chickens to sell or to gather eggs for sale, she made natural yoghurt and she never had time to sit and do nothing. Idleness was her arch-enemy and she taught everyone who came in contact with her to work hard. She was a Proverbs 31:27 woman to a T:

> *She watches over the affairs of her household and does not eat the bread of idleness*

Because of these two women I also find it had to sit still for long. I am not used to that. As a result I tend to have four or five things going at the same time, I have to keep busy all the time.

You also teach us about industry, about the benefits of hard work. The bible tells us that there is profit in all labour (Proverbs 14:23), in working hard. Yet there are many people whose hard work consists of lifting the remote control to change channels and of complaining when they are not rewarded for the big hole they have indented in their couch. Technology has turned us into button-pressing slobs as everything has become increasingly effortless. If something requires work, people are not willing to do it. We are now surrounded by people who want the product but are not willing to fuel the reactants into the process of change they need to go through.

Buy you teach us to work, to be pioneers, to stay healthy and to be fit for the mountains we need to conquer and subdue. You teach us to go after our inheritance, after whatever it is that God has already given us which we need to take possession of be it health, wealth, land, money, marriage, family, business or whatever it is that has our name on it. You teach us that our possessions won't come walking home to us, but that there is the expectation of us going and staking a claim like you did to Joshua in Joshua 14.

If we listened to what you are saying, the poor would not sit at home with their hands stretched out to receive, the sick would not sit around waiting to die, the single would not allow themselves to become wallflowers on the shelf, the hungry would not look to their governments to feed them each year, the foolish and ignorant would not wait for wisdom to come looking for them. Instead we would all approach the Joshuas in our situations and let them know that we know Gods promises to us (2 Corinthians 1:20) and we would all be staking a claim to what we know is ours. You did.

Thank you Caleb for teaching us about longevity, industry, fearlessness, boldness and courage. I appreciate your lessons on persistence and consistency, honour and truth. You make it fashionable to be a trail-blazer and a pioneer and you teach us that travelling the well-travelled road is not necessarily God's will for us. Retirement is not for me, I will remain active and productive till I am an old woman and I embrace this lovely scripture in Psalm 92 which reminds me of you and just as it applies to you, I claim it also that it applies to me and refers to who I am and who I will be in 30 or 40 years' time:

The righteous will flourish like a palm tree,
they will grow like a cedar of Lebanon;
13 planted in the house of the LORD,
they will flourish in the courts of our God.
14 They will still bear fruit in old age,
they will stay fresh and green,
15 proclaiming, "The LORD is upright;
he is my Rock, and there is no wickedness in him

Love and blessings

Fari

LETTER 8

HEY SAMSON,

Sam I thank you for your contradictory life because from it we can glean wisdom as we learn that life can be complicated. Most people's lives are complicated, I know mine has been. We just don't always admit it. But like I said, your life shows us that life can be eventful, we don't always end up where we started heading for and sometimes regardless of how gifted or talented or even how anointed we may be, we make a big boo boo of things and our lives, like yours become complicated.

Sometimes we learn the hard way that we are not all that. That on our own and of ourselves we can't really do much and do it right. It's a good place to be though, a place where you are honest and you realise that you need some help and that what you thought was so fantastic about you is not good enough without God's help and God's guidance.

Strong

Samson you are known best for your strength. Had you lived in this day and age you would have won some 'Mr Universe' trophies for being a man of extreme physical strength.

Strength is good. It enables you to do things those less strong cannot do. It enables you to accomplish things that others cannot. Strength gives you an advantage.

Strength can be physical, emotional, spiritual, positional, relational or financial. It can be demonstrated as resilience and that fight-back spirit when circumstances and situations try to floor you. Yet strength can be abused, can be used to oppress and to subdue those who have less of it.

It is a good thing that like food, like money, like desire and even like love can be turned around to destroy rather than build.

Your strength was conditional though. In a way you needed to stick to certain requirements. I suppose most aspects of life are like that. You keep your health if you exercise and eat sensibly. You maintain a good reputation if you are a person of sound character, you prosper if you are skilful and diligent in what you do. For you, there were some stipulated expectations which you should have kept but like most of us in one area or the other of our lives, you didn't have the discipline, you caved in under pressure and you paid a horrible price for it.

I thank God that I live during a time when we are under the new and better covenant, the covenant established on better promises than the old, a covenant of grace (Hebrews 8:6). There are many things that God covers because of his grace. This is not to say that we sin wilfully because we are covered by grace. Even under grace there are expectations. We don't earn grace nor do we earn righteousness. Yet we also know that God like every good parent has expectations for and of his children. He has a standard that he sets for us, things we know we do or don't do. And when we fail and cross the line, his grace is sufficient to reel us back in in love.

But we do learn about consequences from your life. We learn about cause and effect and realise that when our heavenly father teaches us through his word, the boundaries he sets are for our own good. I know you are not the only person who had to deal with the consequences of his actions. We all do. Unfortunately sometimes other people have to deal with the consequences of our actions too. They pay the price for our foolishness.

An unmarried girl can get pregnant but her parents may end up having to suspend their plans so that they can care for a baby. A couple may divorce but the children have to deal with the stigma and with the pain caused by the decision their parents made. A family member may commit a crime but society can ostracise the whole family because of the actions of that one person. Consequences have a ripple effect and you show that, just like Abraham and Sarah's decision to invite Hagar to their marriage bed also sent consequences down the generations as Ishmaelites became a reality that was never supposed to have been there (Genesis 16).

But strength is good. We are told in Proverbs 18:14 (Amp):

> *The strong spirit of a man sustains him in bodily pain or trouble, but a weak and broken spirit who can raise up or bear?*

Strength sustains, I suppose weakness causes things to break down, it can't uphold or withstand. Financial strength brings security and comfort to a family. Spiritual strength can do the same as parents stand and pray, fast and decree and cover their children spiritually. I experienced this from my parents, particularly my mother. I always knew that I was covered, she prayed for each of us, for her grandkids and for her extended family persistently. My father is the same at 91. We are all mentioned by name and brought ceaselessly before the Throne of Grace. Their spiritual strength has not just sustained them, it has sustained us all.

So strength is a good thing. We all need to build up strength and stamina in various aspects of our lives; emotionally, relationally, spiritually, financially and physically. We all want strong people in our lives, people we can lean on in our times of weakness, people who can speak life into us when we are not able to do so for ourselves. We all need strong people that we can stand back to back with and face and overcome the enemy.

Two is better than one for this reason and Ecclesiastes 4:9-12 expounds on this fact:

> *9 Two are better than one, because they have a good return for their labor: 10 If either of them falls down, one can help the other up. But pity anyone who falls and has no one to help them up. 11 Also, if two lie down together, they will keep warm. But how can one keep warm alone? 12 Though one may be overpowered, two can defend themselves. A cord of three strands is not quickly broken*

It's horrible when you are married to someone who is weak financially, in health, spiritually, physically or emotionally. They make you carry them and the burden becomes too heavy. Christ tells us to cast our burdens onto him because he cares for us (Psalm 55:22; 1 Peter 5:7). What do you do when a person who is supposed to be one with you becomes heavy luggage? There are situations people cannot help like illness. But there are others where people are plain lazy and just want to be carried on another's back. What is supposed to be a symbiotic relationship then becomes parasitic and it drains. So strength is good and it appears you had it in abundance, the physical kind that is and you performed amazing feats (Judges 13-16).

High price

People envied your strength and feared you because you were strong. You were different and people don't always like that. They try to make you toe the line and be like everyone else or they envy your strength or your uniqueness. So they set out to bring you down from what they considered your high horse and they used tried and tested methods, they used your weak spot, the woman in your life. People say that everyone can be bought, everyone has something or someone that can make them forget who they are, for you, your wife and her pining and whining became your undoing (Judges 13). The person closest to you became your worst and most damaging enemy. The thing your parents warned you about, the thing you knew God didn't want you to do but you wanted it so desperately, that became the instrument of your downfall (Judges 16).

How many times did God say there should not be intermarriage between his children and the world (Deuteronomy 7:3)? How often do parents even in this generation tell their children not to be friends with a particular person, not to go out with a particular group, not to drink smoke or skip school? Yet the more parents speak sometimes the more children and young adults seem to rebel.

You did the same (Judges 14). Like you young people don't realise that the enemy knows that once a parent/child relationship is damaged that child loses a vital support and nurturing system. The enemy wants to make sure that children's ears are tilted towards harmful, foolish, damaging and irresponsible role models. It's like a fruit that breaks off the branch before time. It never reaches its full maturity so it never becomes what it was meant to be. Unfortunately, like you, a lot of young people decide that they know more than their parents. The same people who gave birth to them and sacrificed everything they could to raise them suddenly become ignorant and a source of shame to the very children they gave everything to and for.

Can't you just see Christ hanging on the cross with his arms outstretched surrendering his very life for us and then people use his name as a swear word, or people regard worshiping him as out of fashion. But what a price children pay when they break away from parental guidance, what a price you paid for following and succumbing to your youthful lusts, what a price the world is paying even now for turning its back on the Holy one of Israel (Isaiah 12:6).

Miracle baby

In Judges 13 we learn that your parents were childless but the Lord spoke to them about you before you were even in your mother's womb. He had your whole life mapped out, his plans for you spelt out. This is what was said about you to your mother in verse 5:

> *......a son whose head is never to be touched by a razor because the boy is to be a Nazirite, dedicated to God from the womb. He will take the lead in delivering Israel from the hands of the Philistines*

Not many of us have our futures written out and given audibly to our parents like you. God spelt out how you were to be raised and what his plans were for you, what you were going to achieve and your role in saving Israel. Even though God may not have spoken audibly to our parents, he has made sure that his word is there to guide them regarding each child. Every child is a blessing and a miracle (Psalm 127:3). Every child comes from God who created and moulded us (Jeremiah 1:5; Isaiah 49). God's plans for us are for good and not evil (Jeremiah 29:11) and he has given each parent guidelines on how to train their children the way they should go (Proverbs 22:6), so none of us can say that God didn't speak, he did, we may just have been too busy or too proud to listen and to hear.

Looking at your life we also learn important lessons about God and about our will. God made plans for you but he gave you the free will to either go along with his plans for you which are plans to prosper you and not to harm you (Jeremiah 29:11) or to decide to go a different way like you did.

It's amazing how easily people blame God when things go wrong. I would like to ask each of us if we ever asked God what his plans were and are for us. I would like to look every grumbler in the eye and ask if they ever checked with their creator how he wanted them to live, what he wanted them to do, who and whose life he wanted them to affect and how.

If we each took time to talk to God, to read his word, to pray and find out what he wants us to do then we could go back to him if we were struggling, we would be justified for going back and sharing our struggles. But if like you Samson we toss his plans for us aside and decided that we are cleverer than him and want to do things differently, then how dare we complain when our plans fail? If we make ourselves lords of our lives then what does God have to do with our failure and how can we blame him when our sand castles collapse around us?

So we are all miracle babies in our own way, there were celebrations when we were born, I know my dignified dad is said to have danced in the street at my birth. So even if our parents may not have acknowledged our birth with a celebration we know without a doubt that we are a miracle that was brought to their door. We know also that God has amazing plans for us and that he called us to our purposes even before our birth, check Isaiah 49. What is left therefore is for us to take our miracle selves to the throne of Grace, approaching it boldly of course (Hebrews 4:16) and ask our Father what he wants us to do with our lives.

Off kilter!

Your life seems a bit askew, a bit off kilter or out of balance because of its contradictions. Yet maybe it is from this that we learn that it is not by might or by power (Zechariah 4:6), we learn not to trust in chariots and horses (Psalm 20:7) and we learn also not to rely on the arm of flesh (2 Chronicles 32:8). Physical strength does not necessarily mean spiritual strength or intelligence. You were so strong physically so one would be forgiven for expecting a balance. One would also assume that your strength in resisting temptation would also be equally great.

I'm just reading Judges 15 and 16 again and as I read, it would be so easy to judge you and condemn you for your actions and your rather temperamental and tempestuous character. But if each of us reads about your life with honest eyes, we realise that at some point in our lives we have also led lives of contradiction. We have also known that we are called of God but we have behaved in ways that did not reflect our destiny. So as Christ said, let him, that has no sin cast the first stone (John 8:7).

Even though we don't judge least we also be judged (James 5:8) yet we still need to learn and to be warned off certain behaviour as we look at the consequences of yours. Forgive me for spreading your life out like a sheet, but I am sure you know I don't do it to condemn but rather to milk and draw from it lessons that will encourage, reprove, correct, instruct and equip (2 Timothy 3:16) whoever read and responds to the stirrings of God's Holy Spirit within them.

The contradiction for me comes from the fact that you knew you were a servant of God, a judge over Israel, a miracle baby and a man of great strength. Yet you lived your life as if you were none of the above. You were rebellious, vindictive and vengeful, you went into prostitutes and there did not seem to be any boundaries at all around you, you seemed to be a law unto yourself. That's where the off kilterness shows. Chosen by God and endowed with strength yet reckless and weak. Set aside yet hankering after the common. Anointed yet rebellious.

I suppose this is the same problem in churches today when believers' lifestyles echo those of the unsaved, when their marriages are as temporal and difficult, when their families are as dysfunctional, when their speech is as vulgar and when their lives are as chaotic. There has to be a difference which is why the Israelites were asked to choose who they were going to serve (Joshua 24:15). As children of God we can't have a mish-mash of believing and doubting, righteousness and sin, cleanliness and filth. We have to choose; we have to decide whose we are and live as children of the King, the King of kings.

Contradictory lives destroy testimonies. Sinners look at contradictory lives and there is nothing there to make them want to emulate. Your strength became a weapon of violence and destruction and that coupled with your relationship issues marred your testimony.

Your issue with Delilah is sad because in so many ways it reminds me of issues I have had to put a stop to. It brings back recollections of repetitive mistakes and cyclic choices I made which I shouldn't have. The devil is deceitful and sly. He knows what each person's weaknesses are and he presses that button unashamedly. Look at what happened in Judges 14:17. You yielded to a manipulative woman and lives were lost because of that weakness. In Judges 16:16 we see yet again, another nagging woman that you couldn't withstand and you succumbed to the pressure and lost your hair, your sight, your dignity, your testimony and your freedom.

It's so important to find a way to cover and shield our weak places so that the enemy doesn't destroy us through them. Good friends, and the operative word here is 'good', are crucial for this. They can steer us away from the drink, the men, the women, the drugs and everything else that wants to destroy our credibility. Accountability to someone you respect can be a crucial lifeline as is setting boundaries in agreement with the Holy Spirit and with the word of God.

Looking unto Jesus who is the author and perfecter of our faith (Hebrews 12:2) is a must. He knows our weaknesses (Hebrews 4:15). He knows us intimately because he made us and knit us together in our mothers' wombs (Psalm 139:13). His plans for us are plans for good and not evil (Jeremiah 29:11). Only he can help us in our times of frailty and weakness.

So even though the contradictions might appear, we can ask God to help us and give us strength, discernment and the ability to fight and win against the negative things the enemy wants to highlight in our lives.

Bounced back

The thing I appreciate most about you Sam is not your phenomenal strength or the feats you performed. What grasps me the most is the fact that you went out on a high note. You failed but then you triumphed.

Just when the enemy thought he had got you for real you wiped the floor with him. That is a hope-stirring testimony for anyone who failed dismally in finances, in marriage, in parenting, in serving God or in anything else. You make people realise that regardless of how low they may have fallen, they can still rise up even with their last breath. This verse comes to mind:

To the living there is hope (Ecclesiastes 9:4)

As long as there is still breath in a body the potential to succeed and to excel still remains and if released it will still accomplish whatever that person is believing God for.

Here is another verse from Micah 7: 8 that sums up your life:

> *Do not gloat over me, my enemy! Though I have fallen, I will rise. Though I sit in darkness, the LORD will be my light.*

Reading about you also reminds me of the God of the second and the third, the fourth and the fifth chances, the God who forgives (Micah 7:18), casts away our mistakes (Psalm 103:12) and forgets (Isaiah 43:25). When he looks at me just like he did when he looked at you, he sees us as the best of the best. Our goodness is not linked to works or our own wonderfulness, our efforts and works and attempts and straightening ourselves before him are likened to dirty rags (Isaiah 64:6). When he looks, he sees himself in us, he sees the blood of the the Lamb which makes him see perfection; the redeemed, the forgiven, the washed and cleansed, the righteous children that he created and lay his life down for.

So regardless of whatever mistakes you made, God didn't withhold your strength from you. He is not like people who give then take. He loves us too much to be a tease. The conditions for your strength remained active even when you were in self-destruct mode because of Delilah. God left your salvation in place like he does for us today. He still allowed your hair to grow and added to that the anointing that was already on your life was still there. God's grace remained at work. You cut your hair off (well your actions led to it), but God still allowed your strength to return the same way he had already given it to you, he didn't change his mind about you, he didn't remove you, you disqualified yourself. But when you returned to the Lord (Zachariah 1:3; Acts 3:19), he also turned to you and your strength returned.

So in the end your wreaked havoc in the enemy camp.

Well on that note let me move on. Thank you Samson for allowing your life to be so rich in lessons, rich in warnings and rich in cautions for us. Regardless of what happened you are still an excellent role model mainly because you overcame. Your end wiped away everything that went before. You defeated the enemy even though you were blind and you were a prisoner. You still leave us with a message of both celebration and hope.

Thank you mighty man of much valour.

Love and blessings

Fari

LETTER 9

HEY MOR,

Mordecai I salute you. You are the real deal, a genuine man. When I study your life I see a man who went beyond the call of duty in every way. You didn't just do what was expected you did what was right and what was Godly.

You hated wrong, but you didn't just talk, you did what needed to be done to make things right. You are not like some of the wimps we see today who are all talk. They complain about the economy, they complain about the weather, they shout at their kids or totally neglect them yet they expect to 'harvest' when the kids start working. But you sowed and so you had every right to get a harvest, you didn't even have to demand it, it came because the word of God does not return to him void, it does what it was sent to do (Isaiah 55:11). And we know also that as long as this earth shall be there will always be seed time which is a time of sowing time, love, money, kindness and everything else, and proceeding after that will be our time of reaping (Genesis 8:22), of harvesting what we planted which God watered and gave a body to (1 Corinthians 15:38).

You were prepared to stand alone against people in very high places, in fact people who saw themselves so highly that they thought they could alter the course of your life bringing you to an early grave (Esther 5). But God had better plans for you and his will prevailed so fantastically.

Loved those others left

Of all the things you were and the things you did, your biggest success was in the fact that you loved a child whose parents were no more. I believe there is a special blessing for every person who has opened the door to their heart and their house to an orphan. So many children have suffered not because there was no one to look after them but because people who should have loved them didn't care.

I pray for every man and woman, every couple, every old woman or man who has given up or shelved their own plans so that they could care for a child whose parents left either through death, illness, incarceration or sheer neglectfulness. Any person who has cared for an orphan, a sibling, a grandchild, a niece or a nephew, may God reward them and shower them with such goodness and grace that they will know their reward truly is in his hand (Isaiah 40:10; Revelation 22:12).

You loved a child, the very people Christ said his kingdom is made of (Matthew 19:14). You removed the 'orphan' label from her life. You became her cover, her protector. What an awesome thing to do. If only we too could do the same, more so now when so many children are having to care for others at a time when they should be playing, growing up, being taught and being loved. Many have become extremely vulnerable because no adult has given them their home and their name as a covering over them, to protect and deliver them from the elements.

I was raised in a loving and secure home. I knew in particular that my dad loved me unreservedly, as a child I misunderstood my mum's methods of discipline. They were excessive and because of them our relationship was rocky. But I never lacked for anything they could provide. I was taught, I was trained, I was given every opportunity they could barely afford. They made sure my siblings and I never went without food or clothes even if it meant that sometimes they did. They sacrificed for their children, just like you sacrificed for a child that was not yours (Esther 2:7).

You remind me of people who see that there is a need and go ahead and sort it out even if they don't need to, people who give when they don't need to. That is awesome, may God continue to teach me to love and to embrace those no one else will care for. May he cause mothers and fathers to rise up in this generation, people who make sure that it is well with the orphans that surround us; that it is well with the children we see who need us. When we do this God says we do it to him (Colossians 3:23).

Straight shooter

You remind me quite a lot of my parents. I was raised to respect truth and to speak truthfully. My mother didn't really waste her words. She spoke the truth and she didn't like gossip or needless charter. She said what she meant and she meant what she said.

My dad though more diplomatic, in part because he did become a diplomat tends to be lest abrupt but he still tells it like it is. Your dealings with Esther and with the people you came in contact were also very straight and to the point. You didn't use words to give people a false sense of security. When Esther became fearful and tried to protect herself you didn't mince your words but told her not to forget her roots and also not to forget who had exalted her. In essence you let her know that if she was now too important as queen to help her people; the same God who promoted her would just as easily promote someone else. You made sure she didn't become too important in her own sight and that she didn't forget why she was in the palace (Esther 4:14).

I know sometimes people tear others apart with their words. Speaking the truth is not about being harsh or about tearing into people destroying them. Truth has to be combined with love and with grace. Truth is a good thing, it is meant to build not to kill.

Tongue-lashing people is just that, it is lashing, it is equivalent to whipping. It fills people with pain and with fear. There is nothing Godly about inducing pain and causing fear. God has not and does not give us a spirit of fear but of love and of power and of a sound mind (2 Timothy 1:7) so if you are causing fear check who you are working in cahoots with; it certainly isn't the God of love.

But lying and making deceptive and flattering comments is just as bad. Words are meant to cause another to take action, to reflect on what they are doing, to re-think a bad course of action or to be encouraged. Your words put Esther's role and purpose into perspective. You helped her sift through the important and the trivial and you directed her towards an expected outcome that was way bigger than her own comfort.

I think this is where Titus 2 would fit in. In that chapter older people are advised to use their words to cause a change in the behaviour of the younger. They are to speak words that are purposeful and that lead to a change in behaviour and in actions. This is what you also did for Esther. You spoke to her as mentioned in Titus 2:8 with *'soundness of speech that cannot be condemned'*. Thank you for using your words to instruct and correct without destroying the recipient of your advice. Many of us who are mothers, parents, teachers and leaders would benefit from this lesson, from learning to open our mouths with wisdom and ensuring that what comes out is the law of kindness not death (Proverbs 31:26).

Excellent role model

You are a role model for leaders, parents and the general populace. You show that it is possible to be good and to be kind. It is possible to share what is yours with one who may never manage to pay you back for your help. Churches should be filled with the likes of you as should positions of secular leadership.

It's high time good men and women took time out of their very busy schedules and took time to be a blessing. People are so busy chasing elusive dreams, working daily and accumulating 'stuff' that they have no time to stop and share their expertise or share their wisdom or even a bit of their time with someone else. People are so protective of what they have they seem to erect walls around them that cannot be accessed by anyone who cannot fly over the walls. We are all blessed to be a blessings and it is high time we all used whatever God has given us to open doors for those who have no chance to do it on their own.

You teach us about selfless giving, about showing the younger generation that life has purpose and that their age should not be an excuse or a reason for them to flitter away their time aimlessly. Time is not recoverable. Once it has happened that is it. You then move into the next minute, hour or day. You can't recoup the hours wasted yesterday. Responsibility does not come with an age-rating. We all all have the capacity to make life easier for someone else even if all we can do sometimes is smile at them and make their day better.

Rewarded

It is not surprising then to see you being rewarded, to see your seeds of love, truth, honesty reaping for you rewards and a super harvest when you are recognised, acknowledged and rewarded by the king (Esther 6, 10).

Isn't it wonderful when you serve or sow seeds of blessings and you get acknowledgement for it. Not that this should be the motive for what you do, this would lead to pride and arrogance. But it is good to show appreciation for the actions of people around us who work hard to make sure everything works. The king remembered you and publicly thanked you. Your labours were not in vain. This is how the book of Esther ends, not in praising the beauty of Esther or her wonderful deeds, but focussing instead on you:

> *Mordecai the Jew was second in rank to King Xerxes, preeminent among the Jews, and held in high esteem by his many fellow Jews, because **he worked for the good of his people and spoke up for the welfare of all the Jews** (Esther 10:3).*

Thank you wonderful role model. You teach us to love and to be persistent. You are a destiny maker, a John the Baptist that goes before Esther and before us all using your knowledge and your position to make sure and see to it that it is well with us and that we don't not remain in the orphanages of life but rise to to our rightful place in the palace. Thank you.

Love and blessings

Fari

LETTER 10

HEY AARON,

Aaron you are an awesome role model for people in ministry. In fact you are an excellent role model for anyone who has ever had to submit to someone else. You teach us about God's order and God's plans. I really want to get to know you a bit more.

Leader/follower

I know you may probably be surprised that I have included you in this list of wonderful pace-setters because you are more used to being in the background than the forefront. You are that leader/follower person who has power but is not in the presidential seat. There are a lot of dynamics in that kind of situation and many people fail to adjust, adapt or acclimatise, as a result they leave their place because they think the limelight is not reaching them.

You had some advantages over your brother Moses, reasons that many would have used to start their own ministries. You were older than him and you were a better orator since you didn't stammer like your brother (Exodus 4:14-16). Yet you were humble and you followed your little brother. It takes a very strong man to submit to someone they are better than, even if this may only be in their own sight. It takes a confident man not to be intimidated by the cleverness or the anointing in another.

You seemed happy to lead in your own lane. Yes you fell, like all of us do and gave in to crowd pressures (Exodus 32) and you grumbled and gossiped (Numbers 12:1-2) but looking at your life and service in general the times you failed didn't really mar your track record that much, they just showed you up to be a human being.

Many people leave churches because they have not experienced the meteoric rise to the top which they expected. They feel side-stepped and so they leave and go looking for a place where they can be recognised quickly. They are not concerned about their state of readiness; they just want what those in leadership have. So rather than waiting and taking time to grow, to be polished and sharpened, they walk off and go and start things that collapse because their spiritual stamina has not yet been developed fully. But even though you were obviously an anointed man of God, you were happy to serve even if this meant that you were under your little brother's leadership.

Obedient to God

The bible tells us that obedience is better than sacrifice (1 Samuel 15:22). It's what God prefers from us. Obedience even when we don't understand the rationale behind what we are being asked to do. We trust him enough to obey and to do what he says. You learned that lesson over and over again in your life as you led the children of Israel. You saw the reward for obedience but you also saw the flip side, what happened when the children of Israel disobeyed God.

In a way you remind me of Christ who was obedient even unto death (Philippians 2:8). He knew that the cross and the events leading toward it were all going to be painful. He was going to experience shame, agony, betrayal and untold anguish and if there was a way this could have been avoided he would have asked the father for that way (Matthew 26:39). But even though he knew what awaited him, he still went through with it, he still let Judas betray him, still carried the cross knowing what would happen at the end. He obeyed unto death.

In Leviticus 10 is an account of how your sons died and how you witnessed God's attitude towards rebellion and disobedience. They decided to improve on the instructions God had clearly spelt out for the priests. Maybe the way you did things didn't appear trendy or fun enough to them so they tried something new and it cost them their lives. You were not allowed to leave your post to go and mourn your two boys. Regardless of how hard it was for you, you obeyed.

When you listen to people talking especially so after they have suffered loss or are facing challenges they are very quick to blame God. They demonstrate one-sided relationships where one person has to meet the other's needs and is blamed for everything that goes wrong in the relationship. The other party is in no way accountable or responsible for adding value to the relationship. But you knew what God expected of you and regardless of how hard it was, you did your best to do that. So you obeyed even to the point that you didn't bid farewell to your sons.

You are obviously not of the murmur brigade, of the people who don't realise that they can't blame everything that happens to them on other people. Sometimes we forget that some of the things that happen to us are our own fault. Sometimes we need to be delivered from our own selves. One of my favourite sermons that I have listened to over and over again is called 'Delivered from yourself' which was preached by Dr Ramson Mumba. Sometimes things are in shambles because we made bad choices, we allowed fools into our inner circle or we took short-cuts.

Some of the hardship we face in later life is our own fault. We over-eat and become obese. We can't blame the chefs and we can't blame the farmers. We can however blame the hand that kept raising the forkfuls to the mouth. We sleep and don't study then when the exams are hard we blame the lecturer, our parents and people around us and anything else that can be wrongfully accused.

But you didn't blame God for your sons' disobedience. You saw things the right way. You knew about cause and effect and you were not prepared to place the blame in the wrong place.

These are hard lessons. We need to learn to look inwards before we start finger-pointing. The cause of the problems is not always outside. Sometimes it needs to be rooted up from within us so that our vision becomes clear.

Held up Moses' hands (Exodus 17:12)

Of all the wonderful things you did what stands out for me is the time you and Hur held up Moses' hands because he was tired but needed to keep them up for the army to win. He couldn't hold his own hands up; he was physically exhausted so you stepped in and help his hands up therefore playing a crucial role in the victory of the army that day. Moses couldn't have done it by himself. It didn't matter how great he was, there are things he couldn't do on his own, he needed each branch to supply its own strength so that the whole would win (Ephesians 4:16; 1 Corinthians 12:12).

I think many people fail in pursuing their destiny because they have never taken time to ask God what position they should play. They all want to be goalkeepers or quarterbacks, or they all want to be team captain. They don't realise that regardless of how good a 'star' player is, he or she cannot shine on their own. They could be the best dribbler there is but even they need someone to pass the ball to them. If they try to play on their own they will be worn out. We all need to check where God wants us to shine from, be it front middle or back of the line.

Thank you for teaching us that the issue is not to be the front-runner but to be in the right place to supply as a joint or as a branch what the whole needs. What a difference we could all make if we got to know what our true calling was. I believe the reason there is so much mediocrity is because people settle for visible things so that they can shine whether or not they are good at it. As a result they produce half-baked results because they are running in the wrong lane. They forget that the limelight highlight illuminates everything so if they mess up while they are on stage it is even more visible than if they train themselves in the background until they have perfected their trade, their ministry or their calling.

If we would all listen to what God says and get into place even if the space allocated to us appears to be in the shade, we would produce more than average and impact those around us because we would be operating in our areas of gifting.

I know some excellent Pastors who are not particularly good at preaching but are excellent at administrative stuff and maybe at teaching and shepherding the flock. Some shouldn't be allowed behind the pulpit because that really is not their calling or their area of service. There are some also who are awesome preachers and teachers but can't balance that with administrative stuff or with interacting with people on a one to one basis. We all have our gifts and our calling. The gift or the area where you are skilful is the one that will create room for you and bring you before kings, not the one that is in the obvious limelight (Proverbs 18:16; 22:29).

There are a lot of ministries that should shut down. Many that should find a place to submit to and to grow under. There are many full-time workers that should be praying for guidance so that they know where their area of service should be. I repeat, some people should not be allowed behind a pulpit, should never be given a microphone. What they spew out should never assault and accost the ears of God's children. We all need to understand, we need to fellowship with wisdom so that she instructs us on what we should be doing and how. May God deliver us from some of the foolishness that is regurgitated on pulpits. You only need turn on Christian channels to see that some people should have the microphone snatched off them!

Thank you Aaron for showing us that we can shine even as we follow a good leader, even as we run in someone else's vision, even as we know where we are supposed to be even if that is backstage, making things happen from behind the scenes. Thank you for teaching us that there is honour in holding up the hands of God's anointed, in making things happen so that they can do what God has called them to do.

In a way I suppose your life also teaches the submission God expects of wives and husbands which is mentioned in Ephesians 5. I've decided to add the whole quote because verse 21 tends to be overlooked as is verse 24a. Verses 22 and 23 and 24b are well-travelled roads, taught and preached as if only wives are supposed to submit, as if submission is a woman issue. In fact they have been so over-taught that most women regard submission as imprisonment or as some kind of death sentence. But if we read the four verses in context, we realise that they apply to wives, husbands, the church and everybody! You nailed this and submitted not only to God but to your younger brother Moses.

> *21: Submit to one another out of reverence for Christ. 22: Wives, submit yourselves to your own husbands as you do to the Lord. 23: For the husband is the head of the wife as Christ is the head of the church, his body, of which he is the Saviour. 24: Now as the church submits to Christ, so also wives should submit to their husbands in everything.*

Honoured by God

We serve such a wonderful God. He does not neglect or ignore our labour of love, whatever we do he sees and he rewards (Hebrews 6:10). He does not behave like people do sometimes. He does not use people, he does not abuse and misuse people. He rewards and blesses our efforts. His banner over us is love (Song of Solomon 2:4), his dealings with us are based on his love for us, not on what's in it for him as is the case in a lot of relationships.

Your obedience was rewarded in many ways. You became part of the leadership team and God called you by name giving you instructions (Numbers 20:23). Just like he says that he couldn't hide his plans from his servant Abraham (Genesis 18:17), God also did not hide his plans from you. You became part of the in-crowd, the ones he spent time with instructing and communing.

You were a crucial part of what God was doing for Israel. Even your garments were made to God-given specifications (Exodus 28).

> *2. Make sacred garments for your brother Aaron to give him dignity and honour. 3. Tell all the skilled workers to whom I have given wisdom in such matters that they are to make garments for Aaron, for his consecration, so he may serve me as priest. 4. These are the garments they are to make: a breast piece, an ephod, a robe, a woven tunic, a turban and a sash. They are to make these sacred garments for your brother Aaron and his sons, so they may serve me as priests. 5. Have them use gold, and blue, purple and scarlet yarn, and fine linen.*

The rest of the chapter gives more detailed descriptions and instructions on how the garments and items are to be made and what material is to be used. God cared about every detail and as verse 2 says, he did it to give you 'dignity and honour'.

Your labour was not in vain. Your service was not in vain.

Your humility and your attitude to serve led to you being a fixture in the word of God. You didn't end up in Exodus or even in the Old Testament. God ensured that you had a place through-out the history of the children of Israel into the lives of the Gentiles. Your death described in Numbers 20 was not the end of Aaron. True you didn't get to see the Promised Land, and you paid such a price for the times you and Moses disobeyed God. Yet even in that we see grace at work. God ensured that your line continued to serve him as priests by giving instructions for the transition from you to your son Eleazar (Numbers 20:24-29). We still read about you in Nehemiah, Psalm, Micah, Luke, Acts and Hebrews just to pick a few examples. The honour of longevity, of being made a visible role model was placed on you by the Almighty himself:

> *And no one takes this honour on himself, but he receives it when called by God, just as Aaron was (Hebrews 5:4).*

Thank you Aaron. You show us how to shine from wherever God has placed us and called us to serve from. Not everyone has to stand behind the pulpit, not everyone has to serve with a microphone in their hand. Wisdom is knowing what your calling is and serving God from there, shining from the right place otherwise you blind people if you are shining in the wrong place. Not everyone will be a street light. Light is needed in the fridge, on cars, in and outside houses, on planes. We all need to check out where our God-ordained location is and shine from there; you teach us that.

Thank you again Aaron. You are an example of humility, obedience, longevity and a host of excellent attributes we can all do well to emulate.

Love and blessings

Fari

LETTER 11

HEY DEB,

Deb you will have noticed that all the letters I have written are directed at men. This is not to say there are no inspirational women in the bible. There are. But the issues I wanted to address were best covered through a careful study of our Godly brothers.

Having said that though, I simply couldn't close this book without slotting in a sister. You are too precious to leave out. You are a trend-setter, a woman who refuses to allow her femininity to be a hindrance to what God wants to do through her. There are so many wonderful aspects of who you are that refuse to remain silent, and so my dear sister even while I am presenting these wonderful male role models, I am, typical of contrary me going to slot you in there as well and let you shine.

Having grown up as an only girl surrounded not only by three male siblings but also by male relatives I am used to being surrounded by men. I find men a lot easier to understand than women mainly because I don't have much of a reference point for female to female relationships.

But I have found out that despite being a woman raised at a time when female-hood could be a major hindrance to progress, my girlness has really not been an issue in part because my father didn't segregate between me and his sons. I got the same opportunities as they did and even though I went through a crazy time when I became stupid and allowed others to use my womanness as a weapon of oppression, I know for a fact that I can do ALL things through Christ who strengthens me (Philippians 4:13) and I also know that I have the mind of Christ (1 Corinthians 2:16). As a result, not really to be contrary but just to be real, I decided to make sure my female role model was also included, and that of course can only be you Judge Deborah.

What excites me the most about you is the fact that you are not a specialist. You demonstrate that Proverbs 31 really is an attainable set of verses for us. You are a multi-tasking bundle of virtue and I know your price cannot be equated to fallible and perishable things like rubies. You are a true woman of worth, that conglomerate-identity woman who is a wife and a mother, a leader and a judge, a warrior and a business woman. You make it all appear so easy and doable.

Many times as women we overwhelm ourselves by being too busy in the wrong places. We focus so much on being super-mums that sometimes we fail to major on the things that really count. As a result we become frustrated and drained and we burn out before we complete our journey. You don't seem to have had a problem juggling your multi-faceted roles. Whatever wisdom, special grace, anointing or skills you had, I pray that I too will receive them from the giver of all good and perfect gifts (James 1:17).

Judge Deb there is a lot I could say about you but this is neither the place nor the time. I could talk about you as a wife, you as a judges, you as a landlord and land owner with places bearing your name, I could mention your prowess in battle, your celebration when you won, your awesome leadership qualities and your motherly nature. You provide quite a diverse set of attributes that I know I will enjoy exploring, now but in depth at a later date. But for now let me salute you as an amazing role model for fellow trend-setters, mold-busters, box-bursters, prejudice-wipers, bar-raisers, standard-setters, pace-makers and excellence-calibrators. Thank you Deb, you make me realise that it is cool to be a woman and that with God, there is no limit to what I can do, accomplish, fulfil, achieve, attain and complete.

Alongside you my super role model, there are others I not omit and have now also have included:

SARAH

Our mother Sarah remained beautiful even into her natural old age, what a beauty regiment she must have had as she refused to allow her age to interfere with both her attractiveness and her productivity. This precious woman reminds me of one of my favourite verses which is Psalm 92: 12-15:

> *The righteous shall flourish like the palm tree: he shall grow like a cedar in Lebanon. Those that be planted in the house of the Lord shall flourish in the courts of our God. They shall still bring forth fruit in old age; they shall be fat and flourishing; To shew that the Lord is*

upright: he is my rock, and there is no unrighteousness in him. (Psalm 92:12-15 KJV)

Sarah cancelled out the excuses of ageism and sexism. She became a crucial part of God's plan showcasing God's goodness, demonstrating the power of hospitality and generosity, humility, and faith. There was nothing perfect about her just like there is nothing perfect about any of us. But even with her flaws and imperfection, she is a shining star for any woman who has faced any protracted challenges.

JAEL (Judges 4)

Jael is an interesting woman to get to know. She has a few lessons for us in her brief appearance in the book of Judges. She is another female paradox of both femininity and strength, of kindness and hardness, of toughness and fragility. In a way she makes me want to explore Proverbs 31:10-31 a bit more.

From the time I 'discovered' Proverbs 31 a few years ago, I thought it was an oppressive group of verses. In part this was because so many people seemed to want to use it to condemn. It was used as a measuring line to reflect and reveal women's inadequacy. Husbands seemed to quote it and preach to and at their wives about it. I believe in many men's minds this was the only scripture women needed to know and follow. In fact it was as if things were not working out in the home it was because there was no 'Proverbs 31 Woman' there.

But I thank God that he expects us in all that we get to get understanding (Proverbs 4:7). And as I read about Jael I also realise that in all of us God has intricately meshed what may appear like paradoxical combinations, contradictions that don't always make sense but are a crucial aspect of who we are.

And so as in Proverbs 31 and also as in Jael, we see a mixture of apparent weakness and strength, we see femininity and tough business acumen, we see a woman using what God has made available to her to bring victory not only for herself but also for those around her, doing what is unexpected, unladylike to ensure the safety of the people she cares about.

ESTHER

I look at Esther and I feel for her because I can identify with her. So many times we are put in a place as children of God where we are so unqualified, definitely undeserving of his promotion and sometimes we forget where the promotion came from and we look at ourselves again and flinch as we realise that we really are unworthy. But when God promotes us and makes us visible, his aim is not so that we then bear the burden of the new position. Rather his aim is so that we can make his name great, that we can magnify him and cause the world around us to see him not us and our frailty.

For a while Esther forgot who had promoted her and started worrying about her own hide. But thank God she had an awesome mentor who said it like it is. He kept her grounded and he made sure she knew whose she was and who it is that had promoted her from an orphan to a king (Esther 4:14). How many lives are now encouraged and stirred up because Mordeccai did not allow self-pity and self-preservation to thwart God's plans for Esther and for Israel.

RAHAB

Rahab was my mum's name. Two women couldn't possibly have been more different, yet also alike. My mum was a dignified disciplinarian. Yet she was also a very wise woman who would do anything to make sure that it was well with her family. When she died recently one of the words bandied around describing her was 'unifier'. She unified the family by loving people and sharing her life, her food, clothes, house and everything she could with them.

Despite her biblical namesake's profession, she too was a unifier and she sacrificed all to save her family and make sure it was well with them. She didn't need to; she could have got herself saved and left it at that. But instead she used her wisdom to secure the salvation of her family (Joshua 2). Her boldness assured her a place in the genealogy of our Lord and even though the title 'harlot' has trailed her, it is not trailing in condemnation but rather as an illustration of God's goodness and grace. If he could save and promote a harlot, he can do the same for you, for me, for our families and for the people he has connected us to through church, work or family.

TAMAR (Genesis 38; Matthew 1)

Sometimes bad things happen and we are labelled because society does not like difference. Society wants a woman to get married and stay with her husband regardless of what he does or how bad the marriage is. He can hit her daily, be unfaithful, squander all their savings and be as irresponsible as he wants to be. Society still judges her not him. She is expected to stay.

Tamar's husbands died. One was killed by the Lord himself because he was evil. Yet Tamar suffered for this. She was sent back home as if it was her fault that her husband was evil. She was lied to and then ignored and overlooked. She seemed to be the one paying the price for other people's actions.

But if you know that there is a Godly destiny you must fulfil nothing can keep you down. You will fight until you get your breakthrough. Tamar knew that it was in her destiny to be a mother, she didn't want to go out and become a prostitute, she knew what lineage she was adding to so she bided her time and awaited her opportunity. She didn't leave her destiny in people's hands, she knew what she needed to do and she did it!

Many of us have excuses and reasons, justifications and genuine explanations for why we are sitting doing nothing:

- I am too old to…
- I am divorced so..
- My mum never loved me and…
- I was abused so…
- They discriminate against me and…
- I am from …..
- I am not educated and…
- They don't give me a chance…
- My father was never around and…
- They overlook me and..

- They don't like me so ..
- I am sick...
- I can't do it ….

Tamar could have drawn up a commendable list justifying why she couldn't. But she erased every reason and every excuse. She took charge of her own destiny knowing God was with her and she went out and made sure her name was going to be there in that lineage of the King of Kings (Matthew 1:3).

SHEERAH (1 Chronicles 7:24)

One of the aspects of the word of God I love is how packed it is. One doesn't need to read 10 chapters to get a revelation, an answer, a solution, healing or God's help. Just reading a few words can be enough to change a life.

Not much is said about Sheerah. All we know is her inclusion in the genealogy of Ephraim as noted in 1 Chronicles 7:24:

> *His daughter was Sheerah, who built Lower and Upper Beth Horon as well as Uzzen Sheerah.*

Sheerah is mentioned as being responsible for building three cities. One verse introduces us to a trend-setter, a trail-blazer, a woman of destiny, a woman whose name could not be overlooked even while the names of men were being reeled off. A pause was needed to mention her achievements. The Holy Spirit created space to fit in her name in a place where by human standards we could say she shouldn't have been. She *had* to be included.

This is an awesome role model, one who defies tradition, genderism and any other isms people use as excuses not to venture out and do what they should be doing. It's also not just about the excuses people make but also about the hurdles society sometimes puts before people, the justifications for whatever forms of discrimination and marginalisation.

Well Judge Deb I am going to park here and take time to get to know my female role models a bit more then come back and commit a whole book to them, I think I will call it 'HEY DEB!' Thank you for being my inspiration in so many ways.

Love and blessings

Fari

ROLE MODEL OF ROLE MODELS

There is no way I could sign off and say that I have finished writing this book without including the role model of role models, the one who was and is and is to come (Revelation 1:8), the one without whom nothing was made that was made, who was at the very beginning and yet is still here today (John 1:3), the author and perfecter of my very faith (Hebrews 12:2).

Although all the role models mentioned above are wonderful and they are excellent, they are the awesome witnesses from whose lives we learn about love, faith, resilience, persistence, service, humility, bouncing back and all the attributes we all seek for our own lives, they remain human and their accolades are littered with failure. And sometimes that failure detracts and distracts us from the good in them. Sometimes their actions leave us confused wondering how such people can be role models. In us seems to be a balance which is forever weighing the actions of people around us and more often than not leading to us relegating them to the 'found wanting' pile. We forget that lessons in this life journey we are on are a combination of pain and joy, success and failure, highs and lows. We also forget that if the same scales and balances we use to weigh others were turned round so that our lives were placed there, we could just as easily find ourselves on the 'found wanting' pile!

But there is one in whom no fault was found, one who loved us as no other and was such a good friend that he lay his own life down for us (John 15:13), kept quiet in the face of lies and accusations (Matthew 27:14; Mark 15:5), bore all our diseases (Matthew 8:17; Isaiah 53:4) allowed the chastisement of our sin to be laid on his back (Isaiah 53:5), took every curse that should have been on us (Galatians 3:13) and became poor so that we don't have to live in poverty (2 Corinthians 8:9).

The list of who he is and what he did is endless. This is the real role model, the one that role models also look up to.

And so the concluding letter is addressed to the lover of my soul, to my Lord and Saviour, to the one who daily interceded for me (Romans 8:34;1 Timothy 2:6), who redeemed my life from destruction (Psalm 103:4):

LETTER 12

Dear LORD,

Although I have spoken about all these amazing and wonderful people who set such great precedence for us, there is no greater role model than you, Lord. None can teach like you can. None can love like you can. None can tell what was and is and is to come the way you do.

I look up to you as my perfect role model because that is what your word says in Hebrews 12:2 and in Psalm 121. You are my source of help, you are the perfecter of my faith, the beginning, the middle and the end of it. In Psalm 16:5 (NKJV) David perfectly sums up this aspect of you when he says that you 'maintain my lot'.

'Maintenance' can be a financial term as in an absent parent paying maintenance for his children, hopefully without anyone taking him or her to court, hopefully without lying about income so that the payments can be reduced, hopefully also without anyone chasing after them to remind them of their responsibilities.

But you are not that kind of parent. No one needs to remind you of your responsibilities. You have no hidden stashes of wealth that are 'undeclared income' instead you have made sure that we have access to all 'all things that pertain to life and godliness' (2 Peter 1:3) and also to ' all good and perfect gifts' (James 1:17). Because of what you did on the cross, your death and your resurrection, you made sure that we have become heirs together with you (Romans 8:17) so that now we know that the earth and its fullness belongs to our father, and so to us as heirs (1 Corinthians 10:26; Psalm 24:1). You have not withheld anything from us. The wealth gathered by the wicked (Proverbs 13:22) the wealth in darkness (Isaiah 45:3) it all belongs to us. So you financially and materially maintain our lot. You provide maintenance for your children and have given us the very best there is to give, your own life (Romans 8:32). Parents could do well to learn from you.

But maintenance also speaks of caring, looking after something, making sure it is in the best shape it can be. So I know you maintain my lot, my life; the very essence of who I am. I don't have to worry about needing spare parts which are expensive or unavailable. By your stripes I am healed (Isaiah 53:5), my physical and emotional being is kept whole. Your blood that was shed for the remission of sin (Matthew 26:28) has dealt with my soul and also maintains my life, covering me and protecting me, denying access to whatever it is that may want to harm me. You have made sure that healing and health are my portion, that as your child, health is my bread (Matthew 15:21-18).

You maintain my life by saving me sometimes from myself. The enemy has not always been without, there are times when the enemy has been within, as evidenced by wrong attitudes, wrong thinking, bad habits and choices, foolishness. You have had to save me from self- destructing. You maintain my lot and make sure that it is well with my soul (Psalm 116:7). You have also maintained my lot by saving me from the enemy without, from things that others meant for my harm but which you either blocked, diverted or turned around for my good (Genesis 50:20). You have done a Psalm 91, a work of deliverance, protection, saving, covering, habitation and everything else I need to be safe. You maintain my life by making sure that it is well with me.

You are a role model for me even for things I want to do in my life. I can look to you and learn. Many people run businesses which would benefit from being crowd-pullers, from being able to gather people to whom we can either sell our products, teach or publicise our ideas and inventions. Yet many times we are not able to gather people ethically. Some people use gimmicks, others misrepresent the things they are offering the crowds, or they find ways to threaten crowds into submission and attendance. Yet when I look at the times you had crowds around you there were no tricks, no gimmicks and no coercion. You always had people around you effortlessly. I can look to you as my role model for those times when I need a crowd, when I need people to come in response to products I am selling, events I am organising, teachings I want to do or activities for which I need support.

When people came to you they never went back the same. There was always value added to each person, to their physical, emotional, financial, spiritual, social or relational life. Something always changed, in fact something always improved. It's the same even today. Whenever people gather in your name lives change, the sick are healed and situations and issues that were heavy and a burden are lifted. You change lives, you transform lives, you heal lives, you make the impossible possible and you cause hope to be stirred up again in lives that had given up.

Above all you are not influenced by social stratifications. You love people not their money, their qualifications and their places of origin. You are not impressed by name-dropping. In fact the only name that gets your attention is your name, the name of the Father and the presence of the Holy Spirit. Every other name has no influence, it bows down before you (1 Corinthians 15:27; Hebrews 2:8; Ephesians 1:22). Love that. You give us all the opportunity to scale and rise with your help.

If only all the people that are in positions of leadership had the same heart that you have and the same concern you had and still have for the people who gather around you to hear your word. As we read your word we see you in action and see the impact of your ministry (Mark 2:13, Mark 1:45, Mark 6):

- You taught
- You fed
- You healed
- You forgave
- You loved
- You rebuked and corrected
- You changed lives
- You enriched lives
- You encouraged
- You delivered
- Etc the list is endless

Wherever you went, the crowds came and they never went back the same.

I pray for that anointing of attraction so that I can fulfil your plans for me. I pray for the ability to draw people not to me but to your word and to the things you want them to hear, to learn, to receive and to be impacted by. I pray for a heart that loves people like you do, a heart that doesn't judge and condemn but that is prepared to love even those no one else seems to love.

What I appreciate most about you Lord is your consistency, your unchanging nature. You are the same God Abraham trusted in and who didn't let him down. You are the same God yet again that Isaiah so profusely prophesied about. You are that God that David so loved to worship. You arrived to become the fourth man in the fiery furnace quenching even that roaring inferno saving Shadrack, Micheck and Abednigo (Daniel 3:25). You are the same Lord Stephen looked up and saw standing in heaven (Acts 7:55). You remained the same even to temperamental Peter and to the radical convert Paul. It is you that we read about in Revelation, that you set before us an open door that cannot be shut by man (Revelation

3:8). You are the same yesterday, today and forever (Hebrews 13:8). Thank you Lord.

So in all you do you defy the temporary nature of man, the unreliable, irresponsible nature of parents and adults who should be role models. You prove that we can trust you, we can have faith in you and we can entrust and commit our lives and our situations into your hands without fear of being let down and without fear of not finding you in the same place. You are not Reuben who was said to be unstable like water (Genesis 49:4), or like the double minded man whose achievement are minimal (James 1:8). You remain the same yesterday, today and forever (Hebrews 13:8).

I pray for that anointing of consistency in my service for you, in my relationships, in my attitude towards the people you have graciously put in my life.

There is so much I can say about you and who you are. But I believe that the verse that sums it all up is 1John 4:17 which tells me that I am as you are, not in the world to come but right here and now in this world. My task, my homework or assignment is to study your life and learn from you so that I can increasingly become as you are. I can love as you do. I can encourage as you do. I can teach as you do. I don't need to copy and follow the patterns of men, I don't need to emulate the traditions of men or try to fit into their customs. You provide the perfect blueprint for my life and I am thankful that I don't need to second guess myself or flounder in confusion. As you are so am I in this world. What a perfect guide, role model and help.

Finally I have to mention the lessons we learn from you about love, loving people deeply and from the heart (1 Peter 1:22; 1 Peter 4:8). You teach us about a kind of love we are not easily familiar with, a kind of love that is a bit difficult for us as human beings to express and also to receive. You love, you are love. You love and draw close to you people that are generally excluded by others, those socially marginalised. You love people most would rather despise and ignore. You call to yourself the heavy laden and you give them rest (Matthew 11:28). You loved and love indiscriminately and shed your blood for all. You did not love only those who looked or talked like you. You don't only bless those who are good but you cause rain to fall on the just and on the wicked (Matthew 5:45).

I want to go back to Hebrews 12:2 again. This is what it says:

> *..fixing our eyes on Jesus, the pioneer and perfecter of faith. For the joy set before him he endured the cross, scorning its shame, and sat down at the right hand of the throne of God*

Other versions describe you thus:

> ..the champion who initiates and perfects our faith NLT

> ..the founder and perfecter of our faith ESV

> ..the author and perfecter of faith NASB

> ..author and finisher of our faith KJV

Our eyes are being directed to you because you have something not only to show us but also to offer us. The faith by which we must live as children of God (Habakkuk 2:4; Hebrews 10:38; Romans 1:17) actually originates from you, because we know that you gave each of us a measure of faith (Romans 12:3) and also because we know that faith comes by hearing the word of God (Romans 10:17) and we know that you are the word that became flesh and dwelt among us (John 1:14).

You don't have unrealistic, or unattainable, unachievable expectations for us. You expect the best but you don't expect us to do it on our own because you also know our limitations and that of ourselves we really can do nothing (2 Corinthians 3:5). So what you do is give us faith, give us food for that faith, start that faith working in and for us then perfect, complete or finish it. You give us an exam, the questions, the methods, the answers and the distinction mark. Our role is to turn up like Jehoshaphat (2 Chronicles 20:15) and like King David (I Samuel 17:47). The actual battle belongs to you. As long as we turn up in faith, regardless of how miniscule that faith is, it gets you moving, working and fighting on our behalf. Wow! I'm glad to be in *your* army!

The word also tells us that if you are lifted up you will draw all men to you (John 12:32). I wish our earthly leaders would grasp this principle. When you are lifted up, you don't leave a vacuum between you and the mere mortals below. You draw us all up; you pull us up from our lack, from sin, from sickness and the tangles we have allowed to bind us to the bottom, to ordinariness and mediocrity, to religion and ungodly traditions. You don't leave us in our messes; you draw us up and bring us up to where you are.

Like I said, I so wish our earthly leaders, our church leaders, leaders in the home and everyone in a position of authority would grasp this principle of lifting up those beneath. They have been put in a place of advantage and they shouldn't be busy bashing the heads of everyone who is trying to rise up and come onto the platform. As soon as they are elected, anointed, appointed or promoted their primary acquisition becomes a stage-clearing weapon which they aim at anyone who has the audacity to try and come on board.

But you want us to benefit from our connection with you. You want us healed, saved, prospering, happy, delivered and free. Most leaders want people enslaved, doing their bidding, at their beck and call with barely enough to feed themselves and their families and dependant, not in the good way you expect us to depend on you but bound and enslaved. They want that seat on the pedestal for their benefit and theirs only.

A good role model thinks about the people looking up to him or her and wants what is best for them. They are not intimidated by the success of up and coming politicians, business people, men and women, but rather celebrate the increased number of people achieving their dreams, succeeding, breaking barriers and becoming role models as well.

Lord you are different from earthly leaders in that you want us to be like you. You are not trying to keep us down and busted. Instead you want us to excel, to do well, to fly! Your word says this:

> *Herein is our love made perfect, that we may have boldness in the day of judgment: because as he is, so are we in this world 1 John 4:17 KJV*

You want us to be like you. You have no public life and private life. What we see is what we get. Not many people have that level of transparency. Not many leaders can tell people to be like them or hold themselves up as a perfect role model but you do and you are. I don't have to cross my arms to cover my face cowering when I look at you expecting a blow to come and harm me. I can lift my arms up in surrender and praise and also expecting to be embraced in love.

Fathers could learn from you how to be role models for their children. Mothers could learn from you how to love and nurture their families like you do. Church and political leaders could learn from you how to lead sacrificially without expecting to fill their own coffers first then giving out charitable donations to the people whose lives have been entrusted to them.

My prayer is that I may learn from you each day; that I may truly be as you are, that I may love unconditionally and consistently. You are so good to us that you don't just tell us to learn from you, you make sure we can look up to you daily, you have presented yourself as a living sacrifice and you have not withheld anything from us.

Teach us to be genuine and to be sincere Lord. Teach us as adults, parents and leaders to be worth looking at. When our children or those we lead look at us, let them see people worth following, people worth respecting, people worth listening to, people worth emulating. We look to you, the role model of role models.

Thank you Lord

Love always

Fari

CONCLUSION

Many people have experienced negative things in their childhood. Many are not able to rise above the issues, challenges and disappointments and pain they have had to deal with growing up. As a result their adulthood suffers because they carry the burdens of their youth into their adult years, into their work place and into their relationships and marriages.

The bible points us to a great cloud of witnesses (Hebrews 12:1) to people who have lived and whose lives have been found worthy of a mention in the bible. These are people who have faced challenges but have trusted God for their victory. They have messed up and repented. They have records of their highs and lows chronicled for all humanity to see. What I find exciting and encouraging is the fact that the cloud of witnesses is made up of human beings with issues like everybody else. They have not allowed their background to be their reality. If they were blind, they have sought and found sight, if they were lame they have asked for and received wholeness. They have not let the pain of abuse, neglect, divorce, or any other challenge speak into their future. They have found ways like Ruth to deny widowhood and poverty access into their new place of residence.

We are not being told to learn from perfect beings except when we are directed to the author and perfector of our faith, Jesus himself (Hebrews 12:2).

God knows that sometimes we bounce back if we can see a precedence, if we can see someone who fell and arose, someone who failed and made a mess of things but started again and kept trying till they got things right. Humans are funny sometimes in that we don't always want to be the ones to pave the way. Sometimes we just want to follow, we want to walk on a path that someone else has already paved. As a result we look for role models, for people who have already been where we want to go, people who have suffered already to make our journey smooth. Unfortunately the role models pushed before us by society in visible arena are not always positive or truly worthy to be emulated.

The bible on the other hand gives us an unending list of lives to learn from, lives who can teach us through their successes and failures and even from their lukewarmness as is the case of the church at Laodecia (Revelation 3). Our part is to take time to learn the relevant lessons, to take the positive aspects of their lives and emulate them or to beware of the negative traits.

There is no reason why we should consider semi-naked pop stars as role models, neither should the wealth of bed-hopping celebrity cause us to envy or admire them. There is a dignity that demands attention and respect and this is available for us in the Sarahs and the Deborahs, in the Calebs and the Davids, in the Elihus and the Achsahs and in the myriad examples of human and imperfect men, women, children and families that are presented as our cloud of witnesses, our imperfect but perfected cloud of witnesses.

What does your life say
When little eyes look up to you
As they open the pages searching the life within
Should you come with a PG certificate
Clearly embossed 'Study at own risk!'

Can tears dry up be stemmed
Can the gem called hope emerge
As your life speaks possibility into little lives
Telling then failure is but a step
Anything can be overcome

Don't be perfect to be a role model
Be yourself warts success highs lows
Let's learn from your lows gain hope from your highs
Show how you rose from the mud
How you stayed on the peak

©farikanayi 18th November 2013

Contact details:

farikanayi@gmail.com

www.farikanayibooks.com

www.ingramcontent.com/pod-product-compliance
Lightning Source LLC
Chambersburg PA
CBHW020924090426
42736CB00010B/1030